BENEATH THE SURFACE

JULIET CARR

Order this book online at www.trafford.com
or email orders@trafford.com

Most Trafford titles are also available at major online book retailers.

Printed in Victoria, BC, Canada.

ISBN: 978-1-4269-2564-1 (sc)
ISBN: 978-1-4269-2565-8 (hc)

Library of Congress Control Number: 2010901915

*Our mission is to efficiently provide the world's finest, most comprehensive book publishing
service, enabling every author to experience success. To find out how to publish your
book, your way, and have it available worldwide, visit us online at www.trafford.com*

Trafford rev. 3/30/2010

 www.trafford.com

North America & international
toll-free: 1 888 232 4444 (USA & Canada)
phone: 250 383 6864 ♦ fax: 812 355 4082

ACKNOWLEDGEMENTS

I would like to thank God for equipping me with the intellect to write. It has been a long time desire to become a well-known author, with faith and perseverance I'm published and on the way.

Thanks to my devoted friend and former colleague Erma Jones who has always believed in my ability at the start. It was you who inspired me to believe the best is yet to come. I will never forget how you allowed me to interrupt your life so many days and nights with my suggestions, questions and ideas for *Beneath the Surface* as well as *Contorted*.

DEDICATION

This book is dedicated to Clarence, Michael, and Octavia for supporting me. A special thanks to my parents Annie and Fred for nurturing me into the individual that exist. I realize without trials and tribulations there are no stories.

CHAPTER ONE

The South was facing another blistering summer. Only nature's creatures were immune to the hellacious temperatures. It was very much like a summer drought, as turtles crept toward murky ponds and snakes slithered to blackberry brows to coil around shady bushes.

Only a handful of humans were spotted before the sun began its disappearing act. Youngsters were running about with loud orange and green shooters aiming at any and everybody. The clear, cool stream always hit without warning.

The older youth took their time getting dressed after staying up past midnight the night before. They were moving in slow motion. It was usually noon when they began stirring around. Their first stop was always at the fridge for either a glass of iced tea or a homemade freezer cup. After stepping outside, they were like vampires refusing to surrender to the night.

Each summer brought devilish heat to the South but this one was unusual. The billowing steam above the tarmac was spotted with the naked eye. In passing you could see the loud yellow and red tea boxes strewn on the tables of many homes throughout the neighborhood. The sun's rays were so hot that it prompted a creative side to making tea. A large container was fetched and then filled with water. After sitting outside, the sun did its thing. Within a matter of seconds a physical reaction happened. While adding sugar the stirring formed an unusual tango that grabbed the glucose.

Cling! Cling! "Leon, you might want to put down that cup of whatever you're drinking and pass me that monkey wrench. If my memory serves me well, we just replaced the spark plugs and serpentine belt last month. I know this '65 Chevy will run but these repairs are becoming too damn expensive! Tell me again what happened here!"

"Dad, it wasn't last month; it was more like last year. And I don't remember a serpentine belt, so this is a first. It was running fine until the guy driving a red and black Mach I pulled up. He's known for revving his engine like there's something special under his hood. After driving ahead of him a few minutes, this ole baby started wobbling and screaming. Man! That was scary! When I looked back and saw blue smoke chasing me I knew something was wrong. So I crept home slowly and listened to my baby sputter and wail like a wounded coyote."

"What happened to the guy driving the red and black Mach I?"

"He disappeared. Show-off! I guess he got me this time."

"Son, from the looks of this engine you let off enough soot to either blind or suffocate the mosquitoes. That was probably the same day I sat on the porch without being harassed. Usually I have to spray that smelly stuff in the blue can or get some of your momma's *stuff* she claims will run off anything looking like an insect. As nice as it smells I don't see how it runs off anything, but she swears it works."

"We'll have this Chevy working once we tighten this last bolt."

"I hope so, Dad, because a man without a car is a man without a girl!"

"That's it, son! Get in and turn the switch. *Rrrrrr! Rmmmmmm!* Now that sounds nice! Take it for a run, and then give it a shine like the ring I bought your momma when she said, 'I reckon so.'"

"Huh?"

"Never mind, son."

"Thanks again, Dad! Yeah! Next time use your brain when somebody challenges you to a race."

"When I was your age I accepted a few challenges myself. That's how I learned to fix cars. We didn't have money to buy new parts. I refurbished some parts and then went to the junkyard for secondhand parts."

"So that's how you became the neighborhood mechanic!"

"Yep, that's exactly how it happened."

CHAPTER TWO

"Hi, Mr. Jones! Hi Leon!"

"Hello Oletha."

"Hello there, Oletha and friend! How's Ms. Bessie?"

"She's just fine! I see you've got your car running, Leon."

"Yep, just fixed it! Whoa! Who are you?

"I'm Connie."

"And what are you? I, I … mean where are you going?"

"We're walking to the country store for something to cool us off," said Oletha.

"I'll give you a ride. See you later dad!"

"Oletha, why don't you sit in the back and let your friend ride up front."

"She has a boyfriend, Leon."

"I'm sure she does. How can guys resist such a pretty young lady?"

"I'm just showing my home training."

"Thanks, but I'll ride in the back," replied Connie.

5

And who shall I thank for a Christmas gift in July? were Leon's thoughts.

Connie was fair skinned and attractive. Her modest clothes only made her beauty more apparent. She had legs that were as bow as a cowboy's when jumping from a horse to rope a steer with his lasso. She made an introduction that was more than audible for the ears. People in the community wondered how Mr. and Mrs. Davenport created such a beautiful creature.

She lacked the intellect of most, but street sense was what she longed to achieve, and that was achievable while hanging with Oletha. All the bad habits she hadn't picked up at home from siblings she managed to pick up from Oletha.

Connie and Oletha were like two peas in a pod. It had been that way since Oletha's dad split. On a Sunday afternoon after one of Reverend Pete's dynamic sermons, it happened. That day he brought along a bag of holiness, as feet, hands, and bodies motioned to something unexplainable. Ms. Bessie and Helen Davenport met after walking outside. Baptist members were notorious for standing around enjoying a meet-and-greet session following services. They were engaged in a casual conversation when they looked to see Connie and Oletha walking and talking; apparently they met during the youth session.

Oletha was cocoa brown and wore clothes to accentuate her looks, as the guys would say, a "dime piece" for sure. Both the young and the old were restless when she was in sight. Her clothes left nothing for the imagination. They were designed for her curvaceous body, always fitting snug as a glove. Her walk was more deadly than venom forced from a cobra's fangs; it put men in a trance and forced women to look twice.

One Saturday afternoon while window shopping in town, Oletha's orange tank top and faded jeans caused a commotion! As a group of men sat on the tailgates of their trucks eating lunch, they looked to see Oletha sauntering down the sidewalk. Instantly, the nudging of elbows alarmed one another. They could only pause with mouths hanging open.

As one man left a nearby store to join the crew; his eyes locked onto Oletha's backside like a missile locking onto its target. Unaware of his next steps, he studied the subject carefully. Without warning he tripped over the elevated pavement and fell onto a parked car. As his friends laughed, his only comment was "Damn! It should be against the law to tease an old man like that!"

Some of Oletha's hidden qualities were a reflection of her interest in poetry. During eighth grade she became fascinated with poetry after reading some Langston Hughes and Maya Angelou poems in honors English. Her first assignment was the memorization of "The Road Not Taken" by Robert Frost. It had taken two days whereas classmates used the entire two weeks. Oletha was equipped both physically and mentally, from the bedroom to the classroom. People failed to notice her intelligence, as her well-endowed body usually stole the show. The summer months or idle spells often tainted her focus. That's when she tuned in to males, another subject of keen interest.

Other than her usual meetings with males she also made time for church meetings. A large majority of the people living in the area attended Mt. Pisgah Baptist Church; therefore, everybody knew of each other's existence in the community. The church was small, but the congregation was large enough for a chorus of angelic voices. They held the audience captive on Sundays. Reverend Pete could preach the word, but without an awesome choir to ignite the fire of the Holy Ghost, service wasn't the same. The first lady, also the pianist, could force goose bumps to surface whenever she belted a rhythmic sound.

One Sunday, her voice alone caused a commotion, as ladies moved to some kind of inner spiritual rhythm. The men even stood to wave their hands. It was a day gossipers looked forward to other than a day of testimony.

Reverend Pete was some kind of proud as he opened the door of his fine automobile to escort his lovely wife across the lawn. His pride was understandable because she had a beautiful voice and dressed well in clothes that neatly clung to her petite frame. Unlike other ministers' wives, she was well endowed in the areas that mattered most: butt and boobs. It was funny to see men play a childhood game of "freeze tag" whenever she sashayed to the piano bench.

CHAPTER THREE

Connie had four siblings whom she admired, but she often set herself apart. It's a mystery why, because they practically engaged in similar activities except the one in question about his attraction to the same sex. The Davenport children were a unique clan.

Jeff, the oldest, handcrafted the gift of gab. He could talk sugar into releasing its flavor in candy. During one holiday season he met his mistress at a jewelry store. They were picking out a ring to seal their relationship. After arriving at the cashier, he made a small down payment while she opened an account for the balance. There was no way he was letting his wife find out. He remembered what happened the last time.

On a Sunday morning at Mt. Pisgah right after a sermon on Dry Bones, the drama queen saw an opportunity to punish her husband for coming home the night before with a lipstick stain on the back of his shirt. She left her seat, walking down the aisle heavily burdened. After the reverend took her hand she started crying, and Jeff's expression was

What the ...? He didn't have a clue as to what was going on. When everybody got quiet, she said, "Reverend, my heart is too heavy to bear the load."

"Umph!" the women on the motherboard said in unison. Then Reverend Pete asked the congregation to bow their heads and pray for Sister Davenport. Oletha's Aunt had stood and was on her way to the bathroom when she decided her business could wait. Then she started singing, "There's a G-o-d in hea-ven-n-n-n sure will an-swer prayer ..." and the congregation joined in. After the prayer ended the congregation waited eagerly to hear her next statement. Then she spoke loudly but wearily, "Reverend Pete, I need my church family to pray because the devil is trying to attack my marriage." Everybody looked at Jeff. He was sitting back there quietly saying, "Lord, zap me right now. Don't wait for me to get it right. Take me now!" Jeff knew his wife was unpredictable, but this was too much.

The only thing Helen Davenport said to Necie while riding home was how she taught her son to fear the Lord. Then she started quoting scriptures while Connie, Charla, and Necie listened. They had never witnessed such an event. She started with David and his many wives and then moved on to talk about Saul changing his name to Paul after developing a personal relationship with God.

Necie knew about her brother and his many lovers. She had run into him leaving the neighborhood widow, Lena Jackson's house one night. She stopped to give him a ride home. When he got in the car she smiled and shook her head. Jeff then made up an excuse. Necie told him to save it for his wife because she really didn't care. Then he changed his tune and talked about how fine Lena Jackson is and how he's been taking care of her needs since Mr. Jackson expired.

Necie kept driving and laughing at her brother as he filled her in with specific details of a much freakier scene.

Meanwhile Oletha's Aunt Linda couldn't wait to get home after leaving church and start gossiping. After walking inside without putting down her Bible and purse, she began dialing. When the first person didn't answer she quickly dialed another. Finally someone picked up and the first words were, "Guess what happened at church today. Guess who gave a testimony? Helen Davenport's daughter-in-law! Ain't that something?"

Connie's mother was a different story. Have you ever met a churchgoing lady who thought Jesus was on His way back and the minute she stepped out of line He would strike her with a bolt of lightning or scare her to death with a heart attack? That was Helen Davenport! It didn't matter what anybody said or did; her mind was on the Word. It was just sad that nobody bothered telling her it was okay to enjoy life before He returned for collection.

She failed to realize that if she was always doing right, she would miss the opportunity of amusing the congregation on a Sunday morning giving a testimony. There was rumor that some people showed up at Mt. Pisgah for the latest gossip whenever someone stood spilling his guts.

Loretta Stamps, the youth coordinator at church always said there were two reasons in which a man will entertain someone other than his wife. First, the other woman will let him come and go as he pleases. There will never be an attachment as she entices him with some freaky shit in her bedroom. Second, the other woman will tell him he's all of that even if she has to lie about his performance in the bedroom.

As a result, his wife will become a bitter and scorned

woman. Maybe that was Helen's reason for laboring from sunup until sundown, the universal antidote for relieving pain. She was a perfect example of a scorned woman. At the end of her shift, she managed to trudge down the hot tarmac since she never learned to drive. Her routine was simple: check on the children, cook a meal, and read the Word from a Bible kept on the mantle of the fireplace.

If her eyes were ever too weary, one of the children read. This was a striking scene for Mr. Davenport when the children were younger. He smiled at seeing his wife's happiness. Helen gave the Almighty daily time, not just Sunday mornings. "Churchgoers" were their names; they went to church out of routine. She compared it to the routine of putting on underwear—nothing challenging. As for Mr. Davenport, she said his momma was responsible for him knowing the Word.

Connie always said her poppa contributed to the family's craftiness. He was a man of both looks and wit. His speech was smooth as the day is long. When he talked people were instantly held captive.

I bet he wished he could have withdrawn the "friendly fire" after Momma turned into a "yes lady," someone who went along with everything and never bothered to dispute anything. *Gee! What a bore!* The minister should have skipped the line of their wedding vow, "to honor and obey," because Momma took it to the next level. It's not hard to figure out that he's a poor excuse for a husband, the kind you don't want your daughter to meet.

Poppa was crafty, always looking for ways to make more money. His motto: "Man will never make his mark if he works for others and never takes a risk." In other words, man will become permanently bound to his job by the adding of a minuscule amount of crumbs. He will then feel obligated to hang around in hopes of collecting more.

Before you know it man will have reached his golden years mimicking "shoulda, woulda, coulda." It's like the pastor speaking from the pulpit on a Sunday morning" "The graveyard is rich; it's full of dreams and ideas that people never pursued."

CHAPTER FOUR

The unexpected happened with Leon and Connie. Too bad it was Oletha's idea to protect her friendship with Connie. She said it would be silly to lose a friend when neither of them was about to marry. As she often sat and gossiped with Connie about guys from school. She sometimes made up fantasy stories about Leon. It didn't help that he was athletic and had a nice body from working out with the football team during the summer.

"He's not all that!" Connie responded.

"He's all that and then some," said Oletha. "He's got more going on than those guys from Lester County! Where did you find them anyway?"

"I met Melvin at church."

"I should have known. Did your momma pick him?"

"No!"

"Does he know anything other than that farm talk? What else do you guys talk about?"

"Plenty of stuff!"

"Well, I just can't forget him saying, 'I *never* had a drink of *alcohol or smokes.*' My thoughts were bor-ing with a capital B!"

"You're silly, Oletha!"

"I was thinking, '*I bet your penis ain't never touched the hot lava in a love pool.*'"

"Okay, Oletha, but he's nice."

"Nice? Since when has nice gotten someone excited? Does Melvin know how dangerous you can be?"

"Well, no!"

"I didn't think so."

"We haven't gotten that far."

"At the speed he travels, you won't make it by Christmas."

"I'm in no hurry."

"I wouldn't be either if he was the winning prize."

"I bet his country ass don't know anything about the arcane tunnel of wetness. Can you imagine Melvin in the nude with you controlling the swelling of that firm plump pipe that holds the frothy manly juices? Don't forget about the smooth sleek tip that directs the flow."

"Where is that talk coming from?"

"That book I keep in the back of my closet! Guys love how I let those unique words roll off my tongue! They can find any ole girl to yell "Ooh, ah, do it baby, do it!" What's wrong with that? Connie, you need to add a little spice. I have just the book! I guess you know that I don't care for Melvin's boring ass!"

"Why not, Oletha?"

"You're too nice and he'll take advantage of you. I remember him taking over the conversation the night we sat on the stoop, as if his ideas were more important. It took a lot for me to not tell him that he's not the only one with a brain. He needs someone aggressive to put his ass in check when he steps out of line, acting like a know-it-all. I wanted to tell him, 'We're not interested in that farming shit, and our future has no room for it so change the damn subject.' He's probably not smart enough to realize that just because parents farm don't mean their children have to do the same."

"Connie, since sex is your favorite subject, why do you let him bore you with that farm talk?"

"I like Melvin's simple conversations and goofy smile. Besides, you know what they say about quiet people. Melvin's probably holding the grand prize for the perfect moment."

"Yeah, Connie, and you know what they say about exceptions. Melvin is probably the one exception with a bombshell release."

"I'm not gonna let you spoil my thoughts about him."

"Suit yourself, Connie, but don't say I didn't tell you!"

"I saw his car over there on Sunday. What does Mrs. Davenport think about him?"

"You know momma likes any guy who goes to church on a regular basis. When he told her he was thinking about becoming a junior deacon, she said, 'He will be a good husband for you, Connie.'"

"Nooooo! Hell to the no!"

"Who would want to marry such a small-minded guy with tunnel vision?"

"Tunnel vision, Oletha!"

"Yeah, think about it, Connie. In a tunnel there is one way in and one way out. Same with Melvin except there's only one way—his way. He'll pump you full of babies and keep you in the house. Please don't listen to your momma this once. I know she means well, but she's not seeing the picture clearly."

"Oletha, you're too funny! Nobody's getting married."

CHAPTER FIVE

"Let's go walking! We can stop by your Aunt Linda's house."

"Connie, are you dehydrated or something? Stopping at my aunt's house is like going to Bible class on a Wednesday night. And how many times do you see me at church on a Wednesday night?"

"Ugh!"

"Exactly! She ain't saying anything I want to hear. This is the same aunt with two children using drugs and a third one selling drugs. I wonder if she knows that going to church ain't doing them any good. They would be better off hanging with me. They might develop an addiction but it definitely won't be a drug addiction! Besides, the last time I was over there for Momma, she went on and on about my absence at church and how Sundays are meant to praise the Almighty. So come again? She won't see my face today!"

"Oh, I get it! All that talk about Leon got you hot and bothered! Aunt Linda's house happens to be en route to Leon's house."

"Seeing Leon would be nice, but I don't know about that other stuff."

"Oletha, that's all you talk about: sex, sex, sex."

"Since Steve is away for the summer, I don't have a choice."

"That never stopped you before."

"There's a first for everything!"

"Charla, tell Momma I left to walk with Oletha!"

"Hi, Charla!"

"Hi, Oletha!"

"You wanna come walking with us?"

"No, not this time!"

"Bye, Charla!"

"See you later, Oletha."

"Is she still talking to that troll? The same troll that picks up more than garbage?"

"What do you mean?"

"The garbage man's perimeter outlines the cans near the road, not the houses behind the cans. Do you remember the cans sitting out past three o'clock and still full of garbage last week on Ayer Road?"

"Yeah, when the adults thought they had forgotten a holiday!"

"Shaunte said Rufus was at her house."

"Rufus?"

"Yeah, Rufus, the same troll that visits Charla every weekend with the bushy hair and marble sized eyes. His smile and eyes are so obvious that whenever you see him he looks surprised."

"You're not talking about Sister Halle's daughter; the one with the canary voice that sings in Mt. Pisgah's choir! The Shaunte who sings 'Walk around Heaven' with such conviction that people stand, shout, and walk as if they're in heaven!"

"That's the one!"

"Charla is too cute to be confined to the house waiting around on that troll. I bet she'll be the one who imitates your momma."

"What do you mean, Oletha?"

"Nothing, if you don't know."

"Well, that's her choice and her life! I can't force her to hang out with us. She has always been committed to one person."

"Yeah, she reminds me of someone else. I know some guys who would love to become acquainted with Miss Charla and play with that long black hair racing down her back just shy of those cheeks."

"Maybe she's saving herself for the right one, Oletha."

"I hope she don't think that troll is the one."

"Now your sister Necie is a different story! She is nothing nice! I saw her leaving Mr. Sneed's house last week and he's old enough to be her great granddaddy. I thought she was helping Mrs. Sneed out around the house, but boy was I wrong. She told me that after he feels on her breast he gets excited. Then she talks nasty and arouses him to the point of thinking he's having sex.

"Where is Mrs. Sneed when all of this is going on?"

"She leaves when Necie shows up to run errands. Mrs. Sneed thinks it's nice that a young person in the community takes time with the elderly. When Necie needs money she drives him to make a withdrawal at the bank. She says they can't spend all that money in the bank at their age. I told her that it's probably for their children. Necie says they should spend more time with them."

"Connie, I think Necie took after your poppa. So you can never put us in the same category. I do have some boundaries! I have respect for old people and their money."

CHAPTER SIX

"Whew! It's some kind of hot out here! It feels like we just walked into a heat wave, Connie. Let's take the shortcut by Ms. Jackson's house. It circles right in front of the store. Then we can stop and say hello. I sure could use one of the slushies we had the other day."

Beep! Beep!

"Who is that, Oletha?"

"How am I supposed to know? Either we're walking on the wrong side of the road or it's some of those church folks from Mt. Pisgah. Which side should we be on anyway?"

"Momma said you should always face the oncoming traffic. In case a car tries to run you over, you'll see it coming. Yeah, *she would know*!"

"Connie, isn't that Reverend Pete's car parked in Ms. Jackson's drive?"

"Yeah, that's his car. I can spot that long black Lincoln anywhere. He's probably consoling her with some comforting words since Mr. Jackson was buried last week."

"Are you thinking what I'm thinking, Connie?"

"Probably not, Oletha! I can never think of what you're thinking."

"Anyway, I'm thinking we should sneak around back and see what the reverend is talking about. Come on, Connie. I've always wanted to know what people do to console a person after the death of a loved one."

"You want to walk up that long drive and then sneak around back and peep through the window?"

"Do you know another route?"

"But what if he's on the way out and sees us?"

"We'll just speak! He's not the only one with the right to check on the bereaved."

"Yeah, I guess you're right."

Buzzzzzzz!

"Oh my goodness! A bee! Something I didn't expect to see! I almost feel pain when those deadly creatures zip past. I'm glad you momma was home! How could we have removed that stinger from the tunnel of my brother's ear?"

"Yeah, after that I thought Mrs. Davenport was about to buy a car."

"Why do you say that, Oletha?"

"She walked over so Momma could give her lessons after that. Too bad she lost her courage after knocking down our mailbox."

"I was wondering what happened to the mailbox."

"Shhhhhhhh! That bee doesn't see you so pretend you don't see it."

"That's easy for you to say. I was the one stuck in the house with Sammy. His head was swollen to the size of a cartoon character on the Disney channel."

"Stop waving at it, Oletha. You're gonna make it mad!"

"See, it's flying away! Now come on!"

"So what is Sammy doing these days?"

"Same ole stuff, whatever college students do!"

"For the longest time I didn't think your momma noticed Sammy's uniqueness."

"Oletha, a blind man could see something different about Sammy, especially his taste in fashion."

"Yeah, he and I always had a similar taste in fashion."

"Ooooo look, they're kissing! And listen, that's not *Amazing Grace*!"

"Sounds like Al Green's 'Let's Get it On'!"

"I can't believe Ms. Jackson is letting him take advantage of her."

"Maybe she's too weak from Mr. Jackson's death."

"Yeah, and I'm getting weak standing here watching."

"Let's go, Oletha. I've seen enough!"

"Wait, he's at my favorite part, wetting the hard perky nipples. Whoa, she's rubbing on something! Way to go, Ms. Jackson. Check out the prize! I'm gonna scream if she pulls it out!"

"That's enough, I'm leaving!"

"Wait, Connie!"

"I hate that we came around here spying."

"I'm glad we came. Wasn't it cute the way she called him Petey? And did you see that dress Miss Jackson was wearing. Let's go back! I want to see Reverend Pete's face when he releases the manly stuff. That was something!"

"Yeah, something awful."

"At least we know what consoling is about."

"I'm sure that's not how it works."

"Aw, Connie, I'm kidding. It looks like they've been consoling each other way before Mr. Jackson died."

"I heard your brother consoles her too."

"I'm not surprised. Who hasn't Jeff consoled? This isn't a shortcut!"

"Stop whining, Connie, we're almost there. What do you know? I hear a Chevy and see a Leon."

"Are you ladies going my way?"

"Yeah!"

"Hop in and I'll give you a ride. Where are you headed?"

"We're just walking to the store and enjoying girl talk."

"When you finish I can take you as far as my house so the darkness won't catch you. Buckle up, we'll be there in a minute!"

"We're not in a hurry, Leon! So slow this damn car down!"

"Can you turn that up, Leon?"

"What, you like this, Connie?"

"Sure do, it's Sam Cooke!"

"Sure do, it's Sam Cooke," mimicked Oletha.

"Poppa plays his music all the time."

"Do you listen to Sam Cooke, Oletha?"

"Sure, but I prefer Marvin Gaye!"

"We're here!"

Marvin Gaye's "Sexual Healing" was playing as they got out of the car.

"I like that! Oletha stood next to the car singing and gyrating to the music.

"I'll be glad when Steve gets back to put that mouth on pause," whispered Connie.

"What flavor are you getting, Connie?"

"My favorite, banana! You're getting your usual cherry, right?"

"No, I'm trying blue bubble gum. There's nothing more exciting than trying something new."

"If you ladies are ready, we can ride!"

"Can you put that Marvin Gaye back on?"

"Is that okay with you, Connie?"

"What do you mean, is that okay with you, Connie? Did I miss something?"

"Thanks for the ride, Leon!"

"Anytime, ladies! Wanna come in before you start walking home?"

"I guess we can stay a few minutes," said Connie.

CHAPTER SEVEN

"Is Mrs. Jones home?" asked Oletha.

"No, she's still with Grandma up North. You can come in. My dad's here."

"Hi, Mr. Jones!"

"How are you girls doing?"

"We're good," replied Oletha.

"Now whose pretty girl are you?"

"I'm Helen Davenport's daughter."

"Okay, you look like you could be Helen's girl."

"It looks like *The Wheel of Fortune* is holding you captive Mr. Jones."

"I usually retire to this chair after I finish working and getting something to eat."

"Sounds like you have that routine down pat, Mr. Jones," replied Oletha.

"Leon, why don't you ride uptown and get a loaf of that brown bread and some sandwich spread? I was about to fix a sandwich until I found only one bread end in the bag."

"Would you like to ride with me, Connie?"

"I'll stay until you guys get back. I know you want to finish listening to Sam Cooke."

"You're so funny!"

"Leon, don't drive fast with my friend!"

"So, Mr. Jones, is you wife's mom sick or something?"

"Yeah, turns out she's a lot worse than we thought."

"How long has she been out of town?"

"She's been gone about four weeks."

"I hope her mom gets better."

"Well, thanks!"

She's been gone as long as Steve. His hormones are probably raging like mine! That's probably why he's looking at me like that. He's probably thinking about diving into the pool of O. Good thing I wore this sundress! I don't know why I listened to Connie about panties. I don't usually wear them until nature's monthly visit, and of all days, I have on a pair. Well almost, a pair of black thongs Connie gave me. She says it's easy access for her, so I guess I'll find out.

"So, who's tidying the house while Mrs. Jones is away?"

"Leon and I are doing our best to keep things in order."

"It looks like you're doing a decent job. Maybe I'm speaking too soon; the bedroom usually tells the story. Behind which door is the winning prize?"

"The second door to the right!" Mr. Jones opens the door to the bedroom. After Oletha walks in he follows and quietly closes the door.

"Whoa, what a huge bed!"

"Why don't you turn that latch and then join me over here."

You don't have to tell me twice. Mmmmm, he smells like a fresh shower: hot water and dial soap.

The loud colors on the quilt made me think about

being in the park on a sunny day with Steve. My thoughts ended when Mr. Jones turned on the music from his stereo in the corner. Then I remembered the painting hanging on Momma's wall in the front room: *He who upsets a thing should know how to rearrange it.* I'll be sure to straighten up after I get the antidote to soothe my aching body.

I walked over to close the drapes and then bent down to release the straps of my sandals. A picturesque scene invaded the room while my cocoa brown ass was in view. Mr. Jones sat gazing at the string of my thong that disappeared between the two parted semicircles.

"Damn, girl! Bring those T-backs here and let Mr. Jones find that missing string." I turned my ass, twisting up from the floor, and then strutted to him. After my half-bra fell to the floor, I lifted the black and white sundress over my head.

My oversized tits bounced freely as I became excited. The closer I got, the more my nipples hardened. A secret messenger was preparing them for suckling. The same messenger was also preparing Mr. Jones as he slowly licked his lips.

I looked down and almost went into shock after noticing the size of that bulging object desperate to escape. It was standing at attention. As I stood facing him, he grabbed both prizes and stroked them with something warm and wet. He must have seen the sign: *Fragile—Handle with care.* He was handling them like expensive gifts. Then I tried to calm the beast with a light massage, but it raged out of control. When it couldn't handle the movements, I released it. While sitting on the corner of the bed, I stroked it with something warm and moist on top and then lightly underneath.

I rubbed my breast up and down that raging beast until

he forced me to stop. The fluids were trying to escape. After climbing on top, he interrupted my fall as my legs straddled his face. Sparks of flame escaped the tunnel. As he lifted the hood to put out the fire, I went crazy!

Luther was singing to me; at least that's what I thought. When I heard my name I realized it wasn't Luther because he didn't know my name. All the excitement mixed Mr. Jones's voice with Luther's singing.

After walking inside the restroom there were lovely colorful soaps and small empty perfume bottles on the side of the bathtub. The towels matched the soap and toilet paper. Mrs. Jones was obviously a dainty lady. For a moment I thought about a hot bubbly bath with Mr. Jones after noticing the bath petals and beads inside a porcelain vase.

We returned to the living room and sat across from each other in front of the television and continued to watch *Walker Texas Ranger* until I got bored and walked over to change the channel. I plopped down to let the stir lift my dress. After the second time, Mr. Jones demanded that I walk over and sit on that smooth tip. Then I demanded that he wet the rim for a smooth entrance.

I touched the floor with the palms of my hands and exposed my much wanted ass until the aftershocks from the earthquake were gone. After easing down on the tip, I began a stirring motion until the manly stuff came. After climbing down, the dragon breathed a sigh of relief.

CHAPTER EIGHT

M r. Jones and I were exhausted when Leon and Connie walked in smiling. "I hope we didn't keep you waiting too long, Dad!"

"Good thing Oletha was here to keep my mind off the hunger."

"I did hear your stomach rumbling."

"I'll wash my hands and fix your sandwich."

"I'll do it, Leon, since it's late and we need to get home."

"I won't argue with you on that, Oletha."

I called Mr. Jones in the kitchen after fixing his sandwich. He couldn't resist lifting my sundress to pinch my ass. I smiled as a chill went over my body. While sitting at the table I welcomed his fingering. Then he took another position as the running water filled the room with noise.

"See you girls later!"

"Good night, Mr. Jones!"

"Thanks for the sandwich, Oletha, and don't forget to

tell your momma I can replace those brake pads. Leon no speeding with those ladies!"

Marvin Gaye sang as we rode in silence. While they were thinking of who knows what, I sat in the back thinking about Mr. Jones. When Leon stopped to let us out, I thanked him for the ride and everything!

"Oletha, I'm sorry for leaving you there with Leon's daddy. I hope you weren't too bored."

"Bored! Hell, if that was boredom I need to experience that more often!"

"Oletha, you didn't!"

"Like hell! That damn Mr. Jones is a freak!"

"What?"

"If you were on fire and a fireman was across the room, wouldn't you let him put out the fire?"

"But he's Leon's dad!"

"So Leon's dad has fucking equipment too!"

"Oletha, he's married."

"Well, I'm sure his wife can appreciate him being taken care of while she's away. Besides, he didn't fuck like a married man."

"What do you mean?"

"Oh now you're interested! I fixed him more than a sandwich in that kitchen too."

"What?"

"Yes, while Mr. Jones ate that turkey on wheat, I let him play in the pool of O."

"While eating!"

"It was clean; we had taken two showers."

"What? So you and Mr. Jones screwed how many times within how many hours?"

"Oletha!"

"Yes, Connie!"

"So all that water running in the kitchen was to make noise?"

"Right!"

"Leon thought you were helping his dad clean the kitchen."

"What did Connie think?"

"I was thinking, *Please, Oletha, have some boundaries.*"

"I do, just not with a willing and able body."

"I'll probably have nightmares about that man tonight. I can't wait to fall asleep! Call me because I want to hear about you and Leon in the heavy Chevy. I hope your story is as interesting as mine."

"Probably not! You and Mr. Jones have been screwing like two dogs in heat."

"We were feeling like two dogs in heat!"

"Oletha, you have probably scarred him for life."

"No, Connie, he has scarred me for life. I think I'm addicted! If we don't stop talking about him, you'll have to walk me back over there."

"Oops, the lights are on!"

"Where have you two been?"

"Charla didn't tell you I went walking with Oletha?"

"She told me but I expected you before now!"

"I'm sorry momma. We were at our friends' house."

"Were those friends male or female?"

"Momma, we know it's not ladylike to be at a guy's house this time of the night."

"You girls had me worried! Oletha, Miss Bessie came looking for you."

"Good night, Mrs. Helen."

"I'll stand here and watch you home."

"See you tomorrow, Connie!"

"Bye!"

"Hi, Momma!"

"Where are you coming from?"

"Connie and I were at some friends' house."

"Where those friends male or female?"

"Both, Momma, but she was with me the entire time."

"Mr. Jones asked about you."

"Is his wife back?"

"I don't know. I just saw him in passing. He said something about fixing your brakes."

"Oh yeah, he's suppose to be replacing the brake pads on my car."

"I can't wait to take a hot bath and relax. It was some kind of hot today!"

"The weatherman said the heat index was 112 today. Do you want supper?"

"No, ma'am. I'm going to bed after my bath. Good night, Momma!"

"Love you Oletha!"

"I love you too Momma." *And I love some freaky-ass Mr. Jones.*

Ring, ring! "Hello!"

"Hi, Ms. Bessie, can I speak to Oletha?"

"She's taking a bath, Connie. I'll tell her you called."

CHAPTER NINE

It was late in the afternoon when Oletha opened her eyes. *"What the ... this sun is blinding! What time is it? I haven't slept this long since ... I can't remember. I didn't hear Momma leaving for work. That's scary because someone without his hearing aid could hear Momma the way she sings every morning.*

I guess I'll put on my clothes and walk over to Connie's house. She has probably called me fifty times. Is that the mailman I hear? It must be two o'clock. I'll collect the mail on my way.

"Hi, Charla!"

"Hey, Oletha!"

"Where's Connie?"

"You forgot?"

"What?"

"The family reunion!"

"Oh yeah! Why didn't you go?"

"I guess you forgot about my summer job too."

"You must think I'm crazy. I'll see you later." While walking home, thoughts of Mr. Jones flooded Oletha's mind. She couldn't wait to doodle in her journal. After picking up paper and pen she wrote;

The Color of Age

Hues of brown, orange, green, and yellow,
The colors that represent an older feller,
One who possesses both wit and size,
Especially the gift swaying between his thighs.
Does it matter he's thrice my age?

He consumes alcohol instead of lemonade
While flexing his muscles in the cool shade.
His stature can be described as tall, dark, handsome, and mean,
As he proceeds with warm moisture forcing his prey to scream.
Does it matter he's thrice my age?

He's quite the gent you won't find in today's young men
As we sit impatiently wondering when.
Why is nature so cruel in concealing the best
As we search and put many to the test?
Does it matter he's thrice my age?

I've stumbled onto something truly unique,
An older man with an awesome physique.
My first encounter was like winning a prize,
Especially when I witnessed his nature rise.
Does it matter he's thrice my age?

It's frightening to know it won't last long.
Upon her return he'll be reclaimed as her own.
As I endure the rank as loser of the game
I'll keep in mind tears fall when it rain.
Yes, it matters he's thrice my age.

Beep! Beep!

Who's that? I'm not moving because it's somebody for Momma. And they should know what time she gets home.

Bam! Bam! Bam!

Who in the hell is that? "Who is it?"

"Mr. Jones!"

Mr. Jones! Why is he knocking on the door? "Hold on! What are you doing here?"

"I stopped by to tell Miss Bessie I can replace her brake pads tomorrow."

"Is that all you want me to tell her?"

"You're looking good in those jean shorts!"

"I have on some pink T-backs."

"Miss Oletha, you better stop that talk before I bend you over on your momma's couch."

"That sounds like something I can appreciate."

"Ooooo now that feels nice!" *Oh, damn, there's that feeling!* I dropped my jean shorts and Mr. Jones dropped to his knees, surrendering as I lifted one leg to rest on the sofa with the other on the floor, as my butt was planted on Momma's burgundy sofa.

"I better get going. If I stay too long the neighbors will start talking. Why don't you bring those T-backs over tonight and let Mr. Jones finish what he started?"

I watched him walk back to his truck, thinking how it gets better every time. My smile disappeared when Aunt Linda pulled up. I ran to tidy the front room while spraying air freshener and fluffing the pillows. Aunt Linda knocked several times before I opened the door.

"Hi, Aunt Linda!"

"Was that Mr. Jones's truck leaving?"

"Yes, I almost missed him. He was about to get in his truck to leave when I opened the door."

"Well, what did he want? What's that smell?"

"Huh?"

"It smells like strawberry or something."

"It's probably that scented candle in the window."

"Well, what did he want?"

"He can fix Momma's brakes tomorrow."

He must be getting lonely if he's making house calls at Bessie's.

"Is Bessie still dating that man driving the white pickup truck?"

"Who, Joe?"

"I guess that's his name."

"I don't know, Aunt Linda."

"You don't know! Well has he been here lately?"

"No, ma'am!"

"Oh I see!" *Well that explains why Mr. Jones is making house calls!*

"Do you need something?"

"My dryer stopped working."

Your dryer stopped working and your husband fixes everybody's dryer in the community! I bet Ms. Stamps dryer is working. "I'll put your clothes in the dryer and call you when they're ready."

"That's okay, I'll put them in."

While she's putting her clothes in the dryer, let me toss my soiled short in the closet.

"What are you working on?"

"My usual, poetry!"

"Can I see?"

Hell no, then you'll know I was lying about Mr. Jones. Then the community will know he's screwing Bessie's daughter.

"Aunt Linda, I just started this one."

"Well, maybe after you finish that one you can write one for me."

"Sure!" *I can easily think of something about drug addicts and cheating husbands!*

"Do you watch the soap operas?"

"No, I'm not old enough for that kind of drama."

"Well, I'll see you later!"

"You're leaving?"

"If you don't watch the soaps; we can't talk about what will happen next?"

CHAPTER TEN

Connie came from the family reunion in her usual mood. She said it wasn't much fun without me but something was different. Maybe it was my graduation, our last year together at Sainsbury High.

We picked up where we left off and I told her about my rendezvous with Mr. Jones. After I told her how long I slept, her eyes stretched to the size of large marbles. She was totally shocked. Then she danced around me singing that song by The Drifters: "This magic moment, so different and so new but like any other until I kissed you … And then it happened, it took me by surprise. I knew that you loved it too by the look in your eye. Sweeter than wine, softer than the summer night …"

A week before school started, Steve and Mrs. Jones returned and were filled with something exciting. Mr. Jones introduced his wife to what always made me happy and I persuaded Steve to do something that made me happy. Connie and I were having one terrific summer!

Two months later, Mrs. Jones's mom died. As the Jones family prepared to head up north to the funeral, people in the community carried over food and drinks. This was one of the two events when everybody came together. The other was Christmas, a much happier occasion.

Word spread quickly whenever somebody died. One phone call from a member of the church was like the spreading of wildfire. By Sunday morning the announcement clerk in church was reading the time and place of the funeral.

The facts were never clear as to how the person died. While one person stood on the lawn telling how she died from cancer, the next person said it was heart failure. Then another said the cancer was from smoking, while the listener responded, "I didn't know she smoked." Another said the doctor told her about the cancer one day, and she died the next. When it was all said and done we knew someone had died.

Momma and I offered our condolences like everyone else. Connie and Mrs. Helen rode with us. It smelled so good in that car that my mouth began to water. When Mrs. Helen said she baked two cakes and left the other one on her kitchen counter that was music to my ears.

People were so caught up in their routine of work that they rarely baked until the holidays. When Mrs. Helen baked cakes, she put her foot in it. Her cakes were so moist that they dissolved in your mouth like cotton candy. You could smell them baking from miles away.

When we arrived at the Jones's it felt strange to not go in the bedroom. It was nice seeing Mr. Jones again. Since his wife had returned, we saw each other only in passing. Connie whispered to me that she was glad to see the kitchen already clean. Our moms were wondering what was funny after we couldn't stop laughing.

CHAPTER ELEVEN

The soaring temperatures were beginning to decrease at certain times of the day. As the winds began to stir, trees were swaying to welcome a new season. Snakes were being spotted more frequently slithering to opposite sides of gravel roads. Drivers tried to kill them in fear of seeing them later.

Momma reversed her car one evening trying to kill a long black snake. She got scared after Mr. Eazelle, the widower two houses down, beat a snake to death near his mailbox. Thank goodness it stayed there until he got back. He had to fetch a hoe from the side of his house, and he's ancient.

Not only were nature's creatures indicating a climate change, but the falling brown, orange, and yellow leaves were evidence of a new season approaching. Children were raking and bagging to make money. School would be starting soon and Momma said she had never seen me so excited. It was my senior year!

Momma took Connie and me school shopping. While Connie tried on several pairs to make sure her jeans weren't too tight, I did the opposite. I never worried about extra room. The tighter my jeans, the better they fit. We bought T-shirts and had our names spray painted in Sainsbury High School colors: red, white, and blue. We were planning to wear them for homecoming with our jeans Connie promised to design. School would be starting in a few days. It was time for everybody to get their fashions together. Connie styled my hair the night before school. I had no skills for using curling irons after burning my forehead trying to make flat bangs.

Connie's hair was naturally short and her only task was going to the barbershop. It was always a memorable event sitting between four walls of testosterone, a wonder drug for ladies.

While waiting, I enticed the men. I walked back and forth in a strapless white sundress that fell below my butt. My 36DD breasts highlighted the front as they pointed forward from my youth. Connie wore a dark green tank top and white shorts that highlighted her flawless legs. She had a nice pair of boobs too!

The conversations came to a halt until we were nestled in our seats. The silence was broken after I asked a question, and then everybody wanted to talk. A barber passed me the remote so I could watch what I fancied. A customer told us to help ourselves to the watercooler. That was my cue to give them a better look at the merchandise.

After sitting for a few minutes, I got Connie a cup of water and then returned to get myself a cool drink. There was that silence again; the clippers had gone mute. The men stood or sat watching with their mouths hanging open.

A man said, "Now whose girls are you?" Another said, "I bet you two can dance good." Connie never used her five dollars to pay the barber and always left with more money for our sodas or ice cream to walk back home. The barber told us to come every week because his business was increasing with Connie as his customer and me, her friend.

One gent asked if I did private dances. I guess his daddy taught him the dumbest question was the one not asked. He was surprised at my response and asked about our next appointment. Then he made an announcement for everybody to come back in two weeks, same time same place.

While Connie and I were next door talking about the usual stuff and buying sodas, a barber ran over to confirm the dancing comment. After I mentioned money, he said they would all pay. So we set the time after the surrounding businesses closed. Connie said we could do more school shopping. She couldn't dance as well as I could but agreed to a few songs. I wasn't worried about the number of songs because I had a reputation of dancing all night.

CHAPTER TWELVE

Connie and I practiced dancing all week, trying to get ready for the event. Friday night we left the game after the third quarter. Necie was waiting like she promised. She drove us to the barbershop after we got dressed at her place. She gave us skimpy outfits and matching heels.

The building looked empty until Necie drove around back. Then we saw a lot full of cars. Connie and I expected the few usual faces. Someone had obviously passed around flyers to announce the event. Necie said we looked worried and then offered to help.

"But you're not dressed!" She released that one large button on her light pink trench coat. She was wearing a two-piece baby blue bikini for an indoor pool party later.

After the barber opened the door, men were standing along the walls. The barber fixed our music and dimmed the lights. Once the music started we walked to the center of the floor. I introduced everybody and then told the men to get their wallets ready for a night of unforgettable fun.

Then *bam*! Coats fell and noise filled the room after

our bodies started moving. Then I grabbed our coats and danced my way to the side while Oletha and Necie heated the room. All I heard was loud cursing as they worked what their mommas gave them!

The men were too excited to put money on the most profound areas of Oletha's and Necie's bodies. I scurried to collect money that fell to the floor. It was too much for some men, as I watched them twirl their tongues and salivate like dogs.

One man performed "dry sex" with Oletha and Necie. He got so excited his dick spilled over. Another man walked over to Oletha, and she pretended to give him a "head job." I had never been inside a strip club but it had to be similar to what was happening here, men out of control.

On the third song men were emptying their wallets when Necie performed with an ex-lover. He tried to eat of the forbidden fruit as she entertained the audience with a split. When her ex-lover pulled open her butt cheeks and fingered her cunt, the men went crazy. It was one thing to feel a female's body jerking but to see it jerking was a different story! Necie was the shit!

Oletha made her way to the corner and gave a lap dance. That was my cue. I had practiced a couple of dances and the perfect timing was now, a lap dance!

A man almost stripped when Oletha got in a doggy position behind me as we moved our bodies to "Get Up On This" while Salt-N-Pepa sang those demanding lyrics. We had practiced that routine all week. Charla had given us the moves. There was an old saying that quiet people were the real freaks!

We made some nice money! Necie took only enough for gas since her wealthy client was waiting across town. She said aspiring young ladies could always use extra money. While riding home Oletha asked Necie if she missed her ex-lover. "If you're talking about the performance, it was a tease to remind him of what he's missing."

She said whenever a man runs into an ex-lover and later makes love to his wife, his mind is still on his ex-lover; especially one of her ex-lovers. She asked, "Who do you think his mind will be on when he's making love to his wife tonight?"

"You!"

"Right, because tonight was just a reminder of how it use to be!"

It was late when we made it home but our moms were not worried. They trusted Necie to take care of us. She was nice and had a kind heart but she was not the image you wanted in your daughter's head. She was a lot of fun but we knew she wasn't the best influence. Necie was a badass girl we both admired!

Weeks later there were new faces at the barbershop. Some men didn't need a cut but waited patiently for a line, a shave, or mustache trim; they wanted any service that gave them a chance to sit and stare at the merchandise on display. Men are the most precious gifts to women. They walk around hiding the most intricate tools swaying between their inner thighs.

CHAPTER THIRTEEN

Helen Davenport didn't let her children spend the night away from home, so Connie and I were up late talking on the phone. We spent hours in bed under our cozy quilts entertaining each other with gossip about last year's teachers and students at Sainsbury High School.

Connie brought up the time Mr. Thames, our computer teacher, caught me in class with my hand down the tall quiet boy's trousers. Connie still couldn't believe I had the nerve to make that move. She was still asking what got into me!

"Connie, you know how large stiff objects have always excited me." After I heard girls around school calling the tall quiet boy in my computer class Mr. Big Dick, I was curious to see what they considered as big. The perfect timing was the day I sat in class listening to the teacher review some boring stuff about typos and words per minute. My expression must have read, "If boredom kills, I'm dead!" Shortly, he announced, "If you're getting credit for sixty or more words per minute, you can quietly work on something of your choice."

I looked over and saw the tall quiet boy sitting next to me. My decision was to measure the size of his dick. I didn't have a ruler so I decided to go with how much I could grab and hold in my hand. It was big all right! It was so big I got carried away after it increased in size.

It didn't help that his body fell in sync with the rhythm of my hands. We had gotten so caught up that we didn't realize Mr. Thames had left his seat walking to see what was going on since we obviously had not responded to his question.

I was glad it ended with a tap on my right shoulder and a tap on his left shoulder. That was the cue to release the object. It wasn't funny then, but later I asked the quiet boy how he managed to hide such a big dick from me. He just smiled and said, "Aw, girl!"

We weren't the only ones excited. While we were being lectured to, the boy on the other side of me had a hard-on. Later, he said I knew how to talk the shit! He said a few more minutes and he would have messed up his trousers. For the next two weeks the guys in class called me the "silent talker."

After class Mr. Thames lectured to us about inappropriate behavior. He said since it was our first offense he wouldn't call our parents; that was a relief! I didn't do that again because I was late for cheerleading practice and had to run extra laps. The quiet boy was late for football practice and had to run extra sprints.

"Oletha, I can't believe he didn't send you to the office."

"Maybe he was hoping for another hand job."

"What?"

"Do you remember the day I stayed after school to redo my computer project and you hung out with Leon until I finished?"

"Yeah, the same day I thought it was weird that you were happy after an after-school class?"

"While Mr. Thames sat next to me in the back of the classroom, I got a whiff of that nice cologne he always wears. After he explained what I left out of my project, I noticed how handsome he was up close. I couldn't resist reaching down."

"Oletha!"

"It was a nice size but nothing like the tall quiet boy from class."

"Weren't you afraid to grab it?"

"Not really because he was always staring at me. That meant he either wanted me or was fantasizing about me."

"What did he do?"

"He sat there and let me massage it until it went soft again. You know I can work magic with my hands while softly talking shit. I mastered that technique from Necie."

"You mean my sister taught you that!"

"I was good but she taught me how to guarantee satisfaction every time!"

"What about the time Sonja Jackson got caught with five guys in the boys' locker room?"

"Connie, we never could figure that one out, even after one guy said they took turns with someone always on the lookout. That still left four guys to one girl. We agreed that that girl had skills."

"I bet that chunky Mr. Ball, the principal, was thrilled to find them. He probably hadn't witnessed that much action since he was a student in high school."

There was just too much excitement to lie silently in bed reminiscing alone. Connie and I entertained each other for hours. When morning came we were too sleepy to catch the bus.

Momma drove us to school. The junior class went to homeroom while the senior class was ushered into the auditorium. We met to discuss: senior photos, the senior trip, the senior picnic, class rings, senior week, and of course senior prom.

I thought graduating from high school was so far away and now it's only months away. *What will I do without my best friend?* It was time to travel separate paths. I had planned to leave the South ever since tenth grade to attend a university, while Connie had planned to stay down South and attend a local trade school.

Separate Paths

Coming soon, separate paths we'll travel
Only to remember our walks down the gravel.
Now we're reflecting on the last four years.
Never did we imagine crying so many tears.
I wonder how we remained friends for so long.
Everybody at the graduation will hear our song.

Always and forever we'll miss friends and teachers,
Never forgetting the preparation for some to become leaders.
Did we ever think this day would come?

Over and over it kept playing in my mind
Longing for your soul to remain kind
Even though you're a friend and not a sister,
The one I wished from a man called Mister.
How about a friend whom I wish to never lose
And once I've moved on, who will she choose?

CHAPTER FOURTEEN

Mark Poole is in my homeroom and his services are always in demand. He travels up north in the summer to live with his parents in New York. Then he returns to the South in the fall to attend school and to take care of his grandmother who lives alone.

Andrea is Mark's girlfriend, the captain of the cheering squad. I refused to be friends with her because she has something we both enjoy. Nobody suspects Mark's involvement with me other than Connie, who is my best friend and his cousin.

Not only was he in demand with football coaches from colleges and universities, but he is also in demand with the female student body. Steve wasn't aware of his popularity and made the mistake of letting the respectful church boy drive me home after the homecoming game last year when his car was giving him problems.

I remember every detail that happened inside his grandmother's green Buick LeSabre. I sang when he turned down the volume and he requested a song by his favorite gospel artist: Sheri Jones-Moffett. Then we talked about couples around school. I noticed him turning onto a narrow gravel road. He said there was nothing to worry about because there would be no lights shining on us. He said the few houses were occupied by senior citizens who were in bed before the sun went down.

The next eight minutes explained why girls around school were crazy about this smart, neat-dressing, clean-cut, church boy. My curiosity disappeared!

I had always been suspicious of a guy who was focused on his studies and dressed like tomorrow's leader. Temporary Alzheimer's slipped in when I forgot that I was Steve's girlfriend. We were on the backseat when I didn't understand the words rolling off his tongue. He kept saying, *"L'amour de server tu mes dame,"* which he later translated as "I love serving you, my queen."

Now he sits on the second row across from me looking as handsome as ever. I can't wait to meet in our favorite place. If it takes too long, Connie will have to set up something.

Everybody is excited around Sainsbury High because homecoming is next week. We always have a week of crazy events to get everybody hyped. That's when the students have a chance to get involved and support their school.

Monday Memo
To all seniors and juniors of Sainsbury High who wish to participate in the upcoming homecoming events, please pay attention to the weekly calendar and adjust your wardrobe for the occasion. The daily dress code is as follows:
Monday: Peculiar hat day
Tuesday: Crazy sock day
Wednesday: Pajama day

Thursday: Twin day
Friday: School color day

Homecoming was a blast. Seniors will never forget our last year at Sainsbury High. There were so many juniors in peculiar hats the administration started a contest between the juniors and seniors. Connie and I got together every night and put out outfits together.

Andrea wore the most peculiar hat: multicolored made from quilt scraps. The stuffing formed a funnel shape. Leon won second place for best hat; it was made of the plastic binders that hold together a six-pack of cokes. Connie designed it and then spray painted it with unique colors.

Most girls wore mix-and-match socks on Tuesday. Connie and I wore a pair of thick black leotards. She dyed them in loud overlapping colors. On twin day, we dressed alike in faded jean outfits. Connie spattered bleach on the jeans and jacket. The design looked so original that everybody thought we bought it that way. Connie wore a fro and I wore an Afro wig. We won the contest! It was a junior and senior combination. We stood together onstage to receive our prize.

Chapter Fifteen

Andrea and I stood next to each other cheering for Mark as he led the team to another victory. Andrea was your typical preppy girl with sandy shoulder-length hair and freckles. She was also an only child who wore stylish clothes with the right amount of makeup on her already beautiful face.

Guys automatically treated Andrea like a queen. She had it going on with books and looks. I had it going on in the same areas; it's just that I desired something that superseded both, and a reputation to precede all three.

Mark was the starting quarterback, and the stands were packed with fans and college scouts. They were trying to capture his all-American performance. It wasn't enough to read about him in the newspapers; they had to see it firsthand. And did he give them a performance! Mark threw a 90-yard pass; he broke the school's record for a 100-yard touchdown pass and even ran in a touchdown.

I changed into my T-shirt and jeans like Connie and I had planned. I captured the attention of a lot of guys at the bonfire. I felt those piercing eyes of the beasts undressing me in a most joyous way.

The holes in my jeans were cut in all the right places: below the cheeks for a faint image of my butt and a few down the side with the bottom frayed. Connie also frayed the top of my jeans to highlight the rim of my lace thong. We twisted our shirts in back to display the beauty God blessed us with. I never wanted God to feel that I was unappreciative; therefore, I felt the need to expose my blessings.

Connie hung out with Leon, and I hung out with Steve while sitting in the company of Andrea, Mark, and other classmates around the bonfire. We talked about the scouts from different colleges and universities that were in the stands. Then we engaged in more intense chatter as we highlighted different plays from tonight's game. It was a blast!

We were all experiencing a level of invigorating joy until we thought about our friends who will be left at Sainsbury High. We looked at Connie and a few other juniors who were there. It was a night to remember as the guys gulped from their bottles of Jack Daniels while we girls sipped from our bottles of wine coolers.

The evening ended with a few couples wandering from the group. Apparently they wanted to engage in something a bit more exciting without an audience. I was tempted to jumpstart a game of switcheroo, but I knew the girls would reject it while the guys would dread not being able to participate.

If Connie wasn't with Leon, it was Melvin. She was a good girl compared to me. She would never consider such an activity. So I squashed the idea, even though it weighed heavily on my mind. Either guy would have been a great partner for me since I was familiar with each of their unique attributes.

When somebody realized how late it was, Mark offered to take Connie home. Mrs. Bessie was always lenient whenever he drove her home. Steve said it would even look better if I rode with them. After we arrived at Connie's house, Mark and I walked in and spoke even though we could tell from Mrs. Helen's nightgown that she was either in bed or about to get in bed. She wasn't mad when she saw the three of us traveling together. If anything she was probably relieved that Connie arrived safely, especially after the incident involving Tim, Mr. and Mrs. Sam Wilson's son.

It happened after Sainsbury's first away game against our rivals, the Mustangs. We were about thirty minutes from the school when a car from nowhere came around the deep curve on the wrong side of the road. Later we found out that the man was having a heart attack when he hit Trina and Tim head-on as they trailed the bus.

Some guys from school who were also following the bus were able to get Trina out but couldn't get Tim's seat belt to release him. Before long, gas fumes replaced the fresh air, and the spilled petrol ignited.

As the guys worked frantically trying to get Tim's seat belt loose, a stranger grabbed one of the guys who refused to give up and forced him away with the help of another gent. They were out of time. Everyone had to get back before the explosion engulfed the scene. What happened to the slogan: Seat belts save lives? I guess that was the one exception.

It took a while before I wore my seat belt again. In the back of my mind I thought if Tim had not been wearing a seat belt, he would be alive today enjoying his last year of high school. Then I remembered what Connie's momma said: "If the death angel is calling roll and your name is next on the list, there is no skipping a name." Tim's name was next on the list and he just happened to be driving.

As Mark drove me home I asked why he and Andrea had gone missing at the bonfire. He said nothing happened because it was that time of the month so they only kissed and cuddled. I told him that Steve and I didn't go missing because of the excruciating pain in his left arm. "Yeah, that last tackle did it. I'm glad it wasn't broken because we need him for the last three games of the season."

We passed my house and took our usual route down the gravel road to our spot and I finished what Andrea couldn't. After all, a winning quarterback deserved a winning prize. Since he was the highlight of tonight's game, I cheered him on as he proceeded with another winning touchdown. He didn't speak French tonight; he led a conversation we both took part in: game talk.

CHAPTER SIXTEEN

It was time for our Christmas break. The school year always ended with parties, dances, and the exchange of gifts. There was something different, though. Connie and I had not spent much time together. She seemed to be in deep thought and mostly talked about being alone after the graduation.

I didn't know what to say other than remind her of finishing the following year and planning her wedding with Leon. It was time for basketball season to start. Connie and Charla went to most of the home games. Melvin was leading the state in rebounds. I still didn't like him for her but I knew he had mad skills on the court. Even though he wasn't my favorite guy, I still gave him his props when it came to handling the ball and swishing the nets. I always whispered in Connie's ear that Leon was still my choice.

Connie and I went to the basketball tournament during the Christmas break. I teased Melvin about his skills on the court. When he left I teased Connie about him being a lousy lover when it came to private entertainment.

"What if he gets a scholarship that pays for college?"

"Connie, you know Melvin says college isn't for him, and I don't know who can handle the task of convincing him otherwise. I don't understand why he's not interested because he has the grades and the skills. I bet he can't fathom anything beyond this country life."

Signs of Christmas were approaching from advertisements of toys on TV. The older children were folding or marking pages inside the Christmas Wish Book, while adults scurried to buy gifts. People in the community were busily decorating both inside and outside. Neighbors were excited to lend each other a hand with putting lights on lawns and in trees.

The serious decorators put lights and garland around their mailboxes, in the wreaths outside their front doors, and around the edges of their roofs. The smell of freshly baked cakes and pies saturated the community, as women from church hosted a week of baking at each other's house.

I got a lot of gifts, not only from relatives but also from friends. I even received a nice gift from Mr. Jones. That's what I used to buy Connie's and Momma's Christmas gifts. I didn't get him a gift because I didn't want to put him through the interrogation with his wife.

Christmas was a holiday that put hanky-panky at an all-time low. Husbands were either spending time with their wives or trying to recapture lost time with their children, as their guilty conscience reminded them of their previous cheating activity.

New Year's Eve was the last big celebrated holiday for a while. People started early, sitting around drinking sociably and reminiscing. Some brought up goals they achieved while others continued to yap about things they were going to do next year, like lose weight, stop smoking, buy a new car, or find a better job.

The Christians or church folks were getting ready for Watch Night; an event held throughout the South to welcome in the New Year. Most services started at nine and lasted until midnight. I made plans to go with Connie and her family. I had been waiting at their house for about thirty minutes when Mrs. Helen looked at the clock to see it was half past the hour. When Necie finally arrived, she told her momma that she had to work overtime. Connie and I looked at each other and smiled. We knew what overtime looked like for Necie.

Once we arrived at Mt. Pisgah we sat on the same row: me, Necie, Charla, and Connie. Mrs. Helen made her way to the front. Service had started and people were randomly standing to pay tribute to Reverend Pete for his outstanding leadership. Connie and I whispered to each other: "I know Miss Jackson agrees with everything they're saying about him."

The most enjoyable part of service were the fresh doughnuts. There were boxes lined along the table in the back of the room. The coffee smelled so good that it was impossible to pass up a cup. Whether or not you were a coffee drinker you were almost forced to pour a cup and add a bit of cream and sugar to go with those light, moist doughnuts.

Then people started randomly standing to pay homage to the deceased. A lady read the names of members who had expired throughout the year. I missed several speakers because I was busy getting doughnuts for any and everybody in my row. Connie and I entertained each other with rumors about some of the members who stood to testify. We found humor in my uncle's reckless eyes as he sat next to his wife. He had several women to be thankful for, as we spotted two on the same pew. We also noticed Reverend Pete slyly looking at Miss Jackson.

We thought about the scene from this summer after peeping through Miss Jackson's window. We sat mimicking the sounds and gestures of Miss Jackson and Reverend Pete. Necie wanted to know why we were laughing, so we shared the story of Miss Jackson and Reverend Pete. Necie said, "So my brother isn't the only one paying a visit to the lonely widow."

After listening to testimonies from older members, I felt a little guilty about some of my past actions as the congregation was directed to pray silently inward. My heart dropped to the depths below when Connie left her seat to join others at the altar for special prayer. When I saw Charla following, I started wondering how I missed the cue. Necie's expression was saying, *Don't worry, I'm not going up there.* I was relieved because I would have been sitting alone on the bench.

The ministers left the pulpit, walking in a circular path and touching their foreheads with holy oil. The members seeking prayer released enough tears for water in a third-world country. I was hoping Connie didn't give a testimony; if she had, the spotlight would have been on me.

People in the community knew we were partners in crime. I didn't think we had made enough mistakes to stand and testify; especially if Necie was still sitting next to me. She and I were confused by her sister's crying.

I was adamant about the right time to give a testimony, and tonight was not the time. I had always told Connie a testimony shouldn't be given before twenty because that's when adulthood begins. The Almighty is not cruel enough to severely punish teens because we were in a learning mode. The start of adulthood is ample time to get rid of old habits and develop new ones.

The young who expired early were special cases. The Almighty had some open slots for the youth who made minimum mistakes. They were transitioned and collected early while the rest of us were left to repent and change our wicked ways.

I asked Connie if she could imagine the Almighty's expression after reviewing our lives. "There is just too much fixing here! I've got to devise a plane before I can begin with this one." It reminded me of Momma's talk with Aunt Linda about a promotion at work. She refused to accept the fact that she needed more training or preparation for a job in management.

When Mr. Stout, the eldest member of the church, stood to speak, his voice was as soft as a whisper. I couldn't make out anything he said even with the help of a microphone. The Almighty was probably straining too. I scanned the audience to see if it was me and then whispered to Necie, "What did he say?" She shrugged her shoulders to say, *I don't have a clue.*

Then my mind drifted back home. Who was there? Did they eat all the meatballs and chicken wings? I hoped they didn't find my deviled eggs that I pushed to the back of the refrigerator! Momma was having a party, and I was at church with the Davenports.

Momma believed in God but said she wasn't in the mood for spending the end of the year at church. She said last year was enough for her. Watch Night was too depressing and her sins were between her and God.

After service, the Davenports and I returned to the car and occupied our same seats. When Necie stopped at my house, I jokingly said, "I guess we're stuck with each other another year." Everybody chimed in with laughter and said "Happy New Year!"

When I walked inside, Momma asked if I enjoyed myself. I responded, "It was okay, Watch Night as usual." I saw her friends throwing down cards in a hand of tunk while some danced to music and others tried to out-talk each other over the loud music. I grabbed a glass of iced tea and my deviled eggs and went to my room. I dialed Steve's number and we talked until the receiver was too heavy to hold up to my ear.

CHAPTER SEVENTEEN

It was New Year! The community was serious about eating black-eyed peas, corn bread, chitterlings, collard greens, and either peach cobbler or cake for good luck. The menu was about the same at everybody's house.

Connie and I rode with Momma to get cinnamon and nutmeg for the potato pie. She liked freshly baked pies instead of week-old pies cooked during the week and then put in the freezer. When Momma walked to the meat section we looked for the spices. Connie complained about the smells from the deli and how it was making her nauseous. Jokingly I said she was probably weak from the demons escaping last night that the preachers demanded to release her soul. She took off running to the bathroom.

When I asked if her soul felt lighter she gave me a weird look. After we dropped Connie off at home, Momma said she looked pregnant. *What?* "Her color was pale and her face looked fuller than usual." I didn't like what I was hearing. I had to find out if she was still having a monthly period.

Then I thought about Connie crying at the altar at Watch

Night. *We barely talked on the way home. She has another year
of school.*

What about Melvin?

Oh God, Mrs. Davenport?

*I knew Momma was right from the dead silence on the
phone.* "Oletha, I think I'm pregnant because I haven't seen
a sign of anything red for a couple of months. Since the
family reunion I've been screwed up with taking my pills.
I've been throwing up but didn't know what to do because
being pregnant is the last thing I need."

My ears went deaf. Necie always told us to avoid mishaps.
Now this! Necie covered the "ovulating" method several
times. We reviewed the plan so often that Connie explained
it to Charla. "We used a condom during most of the sex. We
covered every road that led to destruction. I'm speechless!
Damn!"

Mishaps

Mishaps are the mistakes that catch us off guard,
The ones that are detrimental if another life is involved.
During our youthful days we engage in multiple romances
As we entertain guys and disregard circumstances.

Sure we're familiar with the opposite sex
carrying potent stuff inside,
The ones serious enough to linger on a nine-month ride.
Too often we mimic we need a little fun in our life.
That's when we say, "Not me, I'm waiting to be some one's wife."

We slip here and there until our bodies feel strange.
Then we remember the missing condom
as our bodies begin a change.

It's then we know that some damage has occurred,
The kind composed of a sperm being transferred.

If not quickly discarded, we chance displaying shame
When nature beat us at this horrid sinful game,
The game of life when we're forced to learn from mistakes,
When decisions of folly don't warrant a congratulate.

The consequences of the **Fragile** *annihilate their youth*
If someone would have reminded them of the truth
As society views them as "sneaky little souls"
The **Bold Ones** *continue to scurry as their story remains untold.*
Mishaps are the mistakes we should always avoid.
We should never let them catch us off guard.

CHAPTER EIGHTEEN

Two days later, Connie came over so Momma could take her to the clinic. She still hadn't talked to her momma. Helen Davenport would demand she marry the baby's daddy, but since he's not from a churchgoing family, I don't know what she'll do. My friend couldn't handle going to school with an oversized belly.

Nobody knew Connie was pregnant. Thanks to the morning sickness, she had not gained weight. She was creative when it came to designing something stylish. Two weeks later Connie told her momma the bad news. Helen was livid and asked Connie where she went wrong. Then she told her to ask the church for forgiveness. Connie thought about seeing Reverend Pete and Ms. Jackson and decided the church wouldn't receive an apology from her.

"I won't stand before those people and ask for forgiveness. They've done worse things and haven't asked for forgiveness. They're not living holy lives so they can't judge me!"

Mrs. Davenport listened to Connie and was silent. She was no stranger to rumors about some members in the church. Connie reached for her momma and cried while whispering, "I'm sorry, Momma." Charla observed the scene and became frightened for her sister. She too had been pregnant. After Necie asked her about Watch Night she made an appointment at the abortion clinic.

"What about school, Connie?"

"Momma, I'm gonna finish."

"You need an appointment to get yourself checked."

"I've had things checked! Ms. Bessie took me!"

"What? You mean Oletha and her momma know you're pregnant!"

"I had to tell somebody."

"Are you gonna marry Melvin?"

"Momma, it's not Melvin's baby."

"It's not! Then whose?"

"Leon's, Momma!"

"What are you doing with that Leon boy? I told you Melvin was a good boy and his family loves the Lord. If Melvin will still have you, I'll keep your baby."

"Momma, what if I don't want the baby?"

"Now, Connie, I didn't raise you to think that way!"

"Then I'll keep my own baby."

"Connie, most guys don't want a girl with a baby, especially when it's not theirs."

"If Melvin loves me, he should love the baby."

"You're right! But think of the shame from his family and friends."

"What if Leon wants to marry me?"

"Honey, his family don't know what the inside of a church looks like!"

"But he loves me and his family will help with the baby."

"Enough of that talk. I don't want to hear anything about that baby's daddy. If he cared, you wouldn't be pregnant with one year of school left. Just think of the shame you're bringing the family. People at Mt. Pisgah will wonder why my children are taking up their father's ways!"

Shame, what about Daddy riding up and down the road with other women and passing you on the road walking! Shame, what about Necie taking an old man's money who is three times her age! Shame, what about Jeff, your oldest son, sleeping around and cheating on his wife! Shame, what about Charla sitting around waiting on a troll that sleeps around with any and everybody! She slipped to the clinic last week to get rid of a disease. Shame, what about your son Sammy liking the same sex! These were Connie's thoughts after hearing the word "shame."

Connie hadn't told Melvin or Leon that she was pregnant. She and Leon always talked about marriage. Most high school couples talked about marriage but never children.

That night Connie asked the Almighty for forgiveness and strength for her decision. Leon was scared to be a father after she told him the news. His parents were upset but knew life was too short to not forgive the mistake of their only son.

It was February and basketball season was well on its way. Melvin still led the state in rebounds. Connie watched him play at Sainsbury High. She was happy but sad. She was happy to see Melvin playing and sad that she was pregnant.

During a booing episode at the free-throw line, he noticed her in the stands. After Melvin caught up to Oletha he found out that Connie and Charla left during the fourth quarter. Leon overheard Melvin asking about Connie and became suspicious. Neither of them knew of the other's position with her. The next day Leon asked Connie how she knew Melvin. He caught her off guard, but she no longer saw a place for drama and told him the truth. He was shocked as hell to hear her momma's plan!

Connie avoided Melvin's calls Friday and Saturday. While sitting on the porch with Oletha Sunday evening, they looked to see him coming down the road. "Oh shit! Connie, where is this fool going?"

"I didn't invite him."

"Well, I'm leaving you two to talk because if he says one wrong thing I'll have to jack slap his ass. I'm sure you're going to be fine with Mrs. Helen inside but I'll stay if you want me to."

"I'll be fine! I'm sure Momma will walk outside once she sees him out here."

"I'll see you later, Connie."

"Hi, Oletha!"

"Bye, Melvin."

"What's wrong with her? I didn't know if you had left town or what. Everytime I call, Charla says you're gone. I was dropping off some potatoes and peanuts at Ms. Mary's and Mr. Eazelle's down the road and decided to drive this way when I saw you and Oletha sitting on the porch. Momma walked onto the porch and told Melvin to take a seat. Then she told him I was pregnant and explained her solution as he sat there looking like a fool since it wasn't his baby. Without saying a word, I apologized and then watched him walk to his car. He didn't look back until he opened the door to get inside. Then he looked at me and mumbled, "I just be damned!"

CHAPTER NINETEEN

Connie was spending more time at home as she and Charla got closer. She revealed the secret about getting rid of an unwanted pregnancy. Connie was shocked to hear that Charla wasn't so naive after all. Then she asked her sister for advice. Charla said, "I don't know if you're ready to be a parent but I wasn't!" Then she said, "It's your decision, not Momma's."

Weeks later while walking with Connie, Melvin came driving down the road. He asked me to give him and Connie a minute to talk. I walked ahead but didn't leave in case she needed me. When I looked back she was going to the passenger side of his car.

He told Connie they were meant to be together. Then he explained it was up to her to make it happen. He said it would be too much trouble to explain the child to his family and people at church.

"I will be graduating soon and I know it will be time for you to have the baby, so think about what I'm saying."

"Yeah, I hear you, Melvin." After he pulled off, Connie

was crying like a crazy person. I ran to see what happened and was pissed after Connie told me what Melvin said.

"Oletha, Melvin is saying the same thing Momma is saying. Other guys might not want me after they find out I have a kid."

"Melvin doesn't know shit! You have a lot of potential. You just made a mistake. It's not the end of the world. Now marrying Melvin is more like the end of the world. Melvin's the one with limited choices. He doesn't even have friends!"

Connie stopped crying and started laughing. "Oletha, you are crazy!"

"Seriously, what kind of guy doesn't have friends? Someone boring, self-centered, and a country bunkin' hypocrite."

"Hypocrite!"

"Yes Connie, anybody who claims to know the Lord and then refuses to accept your child. There is just one word to describe him, HYPOCRITE! He will destroy you. He already talks down to you; if you marry him he will change you from the gentle creature you are. Once you start having children with him, the pain will really begin. He'll force you to pretend your baby never happened."

"Oletha, I'm sure he'll accept my baby once I start having children for him."

"I don't think so! Wake up, Connie! I know Melvin better than you and I haven't spent one night with him. He is not someone you want to marry. He's too overbearing! Think about your baby. He'll put an end to your relationship with her. The older she gets the more she will resent you as a mother. And you love that baby. Did you discuss your plans with Leon?"

"No."

"Why not?"

"Oletha, you know Momma don't care for Leon or his family."

"Why? Is it because they don't attend Mt. Pisgah Church?"

"As silly as it sounds, yes."

"Momma wants to keep my baby so nothing will be in the way of Melvin marrying me."

"Connie, I know you want to listen to your momma, but look at her life."

"Oletha, don't talk about my momma."

"I just want you to open your eyes."

"I'm hurting!"

"Let's get to my house. Momma should be home."

CHAPTER TWENTY

Three months later, Connie had a beautiful eight-pound girl. After the delivery Oletha decided that having children was not for her. She told Connie there was nothing sexy about having a baby.

Connie returned from the hospital with Daphne. Months had passed before Melvin phoned. Helen convinced Connie to marry Melvin and give him more time to accept Daphne. Connie took her momma's advice and married Melvin. As agreed, she left Daphne with her mother.

Leon and his family were devastated about her decision. Leon's parents wanted their son to take care of his daughter. Helen Davenport assured them Daphne was fine and would eventually live with Connie and Melvin.

A year later, Connie called saying she was scared. "What are you scared of, baby?"

"Melvin doesn't want to talk about Daphne. Every time I mention her name we end up fighting."

"It will get better after you have other children. You'll see."

When Daphne celebrated her second birthday, Connie found out she was pregnant. She bought Daphne a dollhouse, and Leon put it together. She made cupcakes and served ice cream to Daphne's cousins and neighborhood friends. Before leaving she rocked Daphne to sleep. While sitting in that chair she remembered past conversations with Oletha.

Connie, just this once, don't listen to your momma. You love your baby and you shouldn't let her or Melvin destroy that relationship! He doesn't deserve you. You are too gentle for a self-centered man like Melvin.

As Daphne got older, she began calling Helen Davenport "momma." She was the only momma she knew. Connie was excited about having another child. She and Melvin were growing close since she was spending less time at her momma's house. She was trying to avoid arguments that would stress the baby she was carrying.

While he busied himself around the farm overturning soil to prepare the land for farming, she kept busy sewing and cooking. She had become an excellent cook after watching her mother-in-law in the kitchen. She and Melvin had lived with his parents before moving into their own house.

Every evening Connie and her mother-in-law were in the kitchen cooking while the men were out working. She learned to milk the cows on the farm. Connie never imagined pulling the tits on a heifer to catch milk in a bucket. The only tits she knew to be pulled were her own when she was alone with Melvin.

As she grew from being pregnant, she took on lighter chores. She picked berries for pies or gathered eggs from the chicken coop. That's when she learned to make that flaky pie crust from watching her mother-in-law. Every week she tried and ended up with flour everywhere. She refused to give up until she could make the perfect crust for a blackberry cobbler.

Melvin never told his parents about Daphne. They had other grandchildren living up North but were excited about having a grandchild living a few feet away. Connie asked Melvin to tell his parents about Daphne. He said things were fine the way they were and she didn't need to spoil her relationship with his parents.

CHAPTER TWENTY-ONE

Years later Connie and Melvin had two children. After she tried to get Daphne to meet the other children, Melvin said the children would be confused. He said if the kids thought she was their cousin, why bother changing it now.

While playing hide-and-seek with neighborhood friends, a girl got upset with Daphne and teased her about not knowing her grandmother wasn't her real momma. The other children laughed and Daphne ran inside crying. Helen said they were being mean and then stepped outside to send them home.

Summer had come and gone but the living arrangements remained the same. Leon's parents encouraged him to move on with life. He met a lady who made him laugh again, and the void Connie left was slowly being filled. Months later her asked her to marry him. She had a daughter about Daphne's age. Mrs. Davenport refused to let Daphne live with them but allowed her to spend weekends.

After Mr. Davenport returned from the east coast and

moved back to the South, Mrs. Davenport denied him the privilege of living with her and Daphne. He built a house a few miles away and came over for supper every Friday and dinner on weekends.

He was baffled at hearing his granddaughter calling him Poppa and Helen momma. After Daphne left to tidy the kitchen, Mr. Davenport said, "Helen, I don't know what kind of arrangement you and Connie made, but you're making a mistake."

"If Melvin couldn't accept her child, she should have never married him!"

"I have my faults, but I would never take a woman from her child and pretend the child didn't exist."

"It's a damn shame that they have other children living with them but can't bring Daphne in as part of their family. And what kind of man comes to visit his mother-in-law and ignores his wife's firstborn?"

"A churchgoer! Isn't that what you call them, Helen? It doesn't take a genius to figure out he's all wrong for Connie. I bet it was your idea for Connie to marry that lowlife! You thought because he went to church and Leon didn't he was the better man. Going to church on Sundays doesn't make a man a Christian!"

Helen sat quietly listening for once.

"Don't you know a Christian can work through a person's faults without harming an innocent child? My grandchild didn't ask to be born. Why is she punished every day? Where is the Christianity in that? Huh, Helen Davenport?"

"I was wrong for treating you the way I did and I'm glad it's not too late to make it right. I can ask the Almighty to forgive me as long as I'm breathing."

"Helen, I'm not asking you to take me back or forget

the past but simply to forgive. While away I thought about how you took the children to church and read the Good Book with them daily. We weren't as fortunate in my house. My momma didn't teach me about the Bible or take me to church. I don't know if she had a Bible. The only time we went to church was for a funeral. My daddy was barely around and the only thing he taught me and my brother was how to have a good time. He said women were all a man needed in his life. What's that ole saying ya'll have at Mt. Pisgah? 'Better late than never'? Well, my never is now!"

Meanwhile Connie was home alone regretting not have taken advice from Oletha, who was away at the university up North. "I'm doing nothing with my life. Absolutely nothing! I'm stuck with this ill-willed man who never considers how I feel. I feel like an egg slowly cracking beyond repair. Oh, God, I hate this life, but what can I do? I have two other children and another one on the way? I'm not happy. My only comfort is pastimes with Leon."

Nina knew Daphne was her sister after hearing many arguments between Connie and Melvin during the nights. Now she was trying to confirm what she heard. She was excited about having a big sister. She phoned Daphne and talked for hours. Daphne was mad at Connie but excited to have Nina in her life.

It was time for Daphne and Helen to have a serious talk about their living arrangement. They mostly cried, Helen for making the wrong decision and Daphne because Melvin didn't accept her. Helen asked Daphne to not be mad at Connie because she loves her.

"I'm to blame. It was me who convinced her to leave you with me." Daphne cried for days trying to imagine a life with her momma. She tried not to hold a grudge but couldn't help feeling unloved.

Daphne remembered the times Connie came over and she felt like a niece instead of a daughter. She never remembered her showing any affection toward her in front of Melvin. Daphne tried to erase Connie's existence. It was painful just to hear Connie's name. She spent many nights trying to picture a life with sisters and brothers. The night always left her feeling empty as tears flooded her pillow. Sometimes she wished Connie had ended her pain with an abortion. Daphne loved her grandmother but wanted a life with her mother.

Daphne talked to Aunt Charla and found no comfort. Aunt Necie said things were handled wrong but Connie is responsible for what's happening now. Uncle Sammy says he told Connie to take Oletha's advice. He knew Melvin was all wrong for her.

"That's the problem with Charla and Connie—they always listened to Momma like they didn't have a brain. Jeff and Necie listened but still did their own thing."

"What about you, Uncle Sammy?"

"I've always used my own judgment because everybody makes mistakes. Maybe they'll realize Momma don't always have the right answer. Uncle Jeff said to move on. Grandfather said I should talk with Connie, the only person who could give me the answer I was looking for. I didn't have the courage to call Connie so I wrote her a letter. She called to apologize after reading the letter. She said when you're young you make decisions that seem right at the time but later causes a lot of pain.

She explained that leaving me was to be something temporary. Then after the babies started coming things changed for the worse. After I mentioned feeling like a relative instead of a daughter, Connie became defensive. That was the day I formed a mental pit to bury Connie. I thought about the time Christmas was celebrated at our house. I watched Connie's every move. I asked her to comb my hair like Nina's. I left to collect my accessories. When I returned she didn't move. Uncle Jeff's wife Tracey said, 'I guess you didn't hear your daughter asking for the same hairstyle that her sister has.'

Maybe she would have combed it if Melvin wasn't sitting there. Aunt Charla took the accessories and then called me and Nina to the back. When I returned I asked Aunt Connie if she liked my hair. I addressed her as a relative since she treated me like a relative. That scene played and replayed in my head all night and I couldn't stop crying. I cried so much that I was sick the next day. Momma put warm towels on my eyes because they were swollen."

CHAPTER TWENTY-TWO

Oletha came home during her summer break. She said there was something different about me. She said I had changed and that she was used to the old Connie who was always positive. Now she says I'm acting like Melvin, speaking negative about everybody and everything. She forced me to change my attitude when she ignored my envious reactions after sharing stories about her life. Then she encouraged me to take evening classes to get my GED.

She drove me to the school and helped me sign up for classes. I hadn't felt so free and in charge of my life for a long time. I wanted to turn back the hands of time. Melvin didn't want Oletha interfering, but she ignored him since he was never her favorite person.

Oletha stopped to visit Helen and Daphne. She left the South with a heavy burden, for the once gentle soul she laughed with for years was gone. While looking out to the peaceful clouds a flood of tears ran as she remembered the hurt and pain of Daphne, an innocent child.

I was about to start school when I found out that I was

pregnant again. Melvin was excited about another baby on the way. I was bitter throughout the pregnancy. It seemed like every time I was close enough to reach out and grasp my dream, someone was pushing it from my reach.

Mrs. Davenport was getting older and didn't keep a close eye on her granddaughter. Daphne knew she could get away with anything; however, she wasn't a typical teenager who was always seeking adventure. She was content with minimal curiosity.

During idle and lonely moments her imagination was filled with thoughts of belonging to a family. She rested with the idea of having a close relationship with her sister since it seemed impossible to have one with her mother.

Helen called Connie to ask if Nina could spend the weekend with them. Connie was outraged at Melvin's response. He said Nina didn't need to hang around Daphne because she's a bad influence.

"*What?*"

"People are saying that Mrs. Davenport is raising a grandchild who keeps late hours."

A silent storm swept through Melvin's home for weeks until he let Nina spend the weekend at her grandmother's. Connie was excited and revengeful that, while dropping off Nina, she ran into Leon. He was leaving his dad's house. His face lit up like a Christmas tree when he saw her turning in the drive of her momma's house.

She trailed Leon to a familiar spot. They sat and exchanged "what ifs." Leon was happily married but still had feelings for Connie. She wanted to tell him that marrying Melvin was the biggest mistake of her life, but she felt he already knew. Moments later they were entangled in each other's arms. It started with kissing and ended with heavy breathing.

It was Friday night; Daphne was planning to watch movies with her sister. That is until her sister informed her that a friend would pick them up later. Nina pulled out a red tight-fitting miniskirt and a black halter top. "Where did you get that outfit?"

"I made it on Momma's sewing machine."

"And she ... I mean they let you wear that?"

"Of course not, that's why I hid it in my bag! What are you wearing?"

"I don't have anything like that but I got a short black halter dress."

"That'll do!"

"Where are we going, to a party or something?"

"You said it, to a party or something!"

"What time does Grandmother go to bed?"

"Ten o'clock! She won't mind us going out."

"You are kidding, right?"

"No!"

"Daphne, you have it made! We can't go anywhere at my house except to church stuff."

"I would trade places with you any day."

"Are you serious?"

"As a heart attack! Momma never takes up for us when daddy says we can't go; it's whatever daddy says. I can't wait to get away from that house."

Daphne followed Nina's lead and hid her outfit under baggy jeans and a T-shirt. After walking into their grandmother's room to kiss her good night, she told them to have a good time. Lights from a car jumped on as Nina and Daphne walked from the house. The door opened to a nice Cadillac that a much older man was driving.

"So this is your sister?"

"Yep, that's my oldest sister." Daphne smiled at being called a big sister as she watched Nina sitting in the front seat playing with the preacher's big nasty dick. *Momma always said, "Don't put anything in your mouth you can't eat." What did Connie tell her?*

Nina didn't waste any time unzipping the preacher's trousers and pulling out that big nasty thing for me to see. I wanted to tell her that I wasn't interested in seeing that thing. But that would have been a lie since I had never seen one so big and up close. She was waving it around like a lollipop or something.

Then she had the audacity to put it to her mouth. He stopped her and said they should wait. Thank God somebody had some sense! He said, "Have you forgotten what happened the last time you licked the lollipop while I was driving? I lost control and steered us in a ditch. Then I had to explain to my wife how the car got a dent. That deer story works every time."

Not only was she a whore, she was a freaky whore! Now where is her home training and who is responsible for that behavior? She lives with her momma and her daddy in a loving home and I live alone with my grandmother. I'm still a virgin and she's a bodacious slut and that's putting it mildly. I don't want her to dislike me like momma, so I'll go along with her plan, but I'm not losing my virginity to an old man. No way!

He didn't announce he was a preacher, but I could tell from the color of his black pin-striped suit, his haircut with a part on the side, and the big car we were riding in. Then I saw a program from church with his picture on the back. It was on the floor of his car beneath his Bible. My sister didn't mind his title; her mind was on the big thing between his legs.

He had the blues softly playing. I didn't know what they were saying but it didn't sound like preacher talk. After we stopped at a house we jumped out and followed him inside.

I didn't know what was on their agenda but I knew what wasn't on mine. My sister whispered that I could make some money if I helped to entertain him. Reverend Wright was all wrong. I watched him walking through the house adjusting the thermostat. Then he said something about doubling up. *Doubling up? What the hell? This sounds like some freaky shit you might see in a movie! She is out of my league. Maybe I should have stayed home watching movies and let her ride this one out alone.*

I liked to dance but not as much as my sister. She had the rhythm and the moves while I had cheerleading moves. I could dance sexy if the music was slow with the right beat.

My sister blindfolded the reverend. He tried to catch us as we ran around the room. I ran like hell around the room while she barely moved. I guess she wanted him to catch her, which was fine with me.

After he turned down the lights, I was invited to my first threesome. I didn't know what to do. Nina's position shocked the shit out of me! I just straddled his belly and moved around like the lady I saw on a movie.

I didn't want to tell them I was still a virgin. But I didn't have a choice; I couldn't massage his belly the entire time. I mumbled, "I'm still a virgin." The preacher grinned and said he had something special for me.

Nina laughed. I guess she knew what he was talking about. I had never seen anybody treat a dick the way Nina was treating the preacher's! I got into it after he lifted me from his belly and put my legs around his head. My eyes began to flutter as he licked my pussy. It felt so damn good!

We made it to the same place at the same time. Nina, the preacher, and I were all moaning. I wanted to ask him to do that again but I was afraid I might have to do something in return. Judging from Nina's behavior, a hard dick was still in demand. She told me to wait up front while they talked.

Three times I witnessed them screwing. While he was lying there trying to calm his breathing, I was praying that his big ass didn't have a heart attack! I walked quietly to the front room and planted myself on the couch in front of the TV.

Once we were safe in my bedroom watching a movie and eating chicken wings and fries, I asked Nina if she was in heat earlier. She laughed and said I should have joined them because she had never seen him moaning and jerking the way he did with both of us.

I asked about their relationship. She said there was no relationship. It was strictly about sex. "So you have no feelings for him?"

"I like him a little, but not as much as that big piece between his thighs."

We stayed up all night laughing and talking about Reverend Wright. He had given her two one-hundred-dollar bills. After I mentioned that the money was probably taken from the love offering at church, Nina laughed and said we did offer him love! I took the money but thought about something Momma said: "All money ain't good money."

CHAPTER TWENTY-THREE

Connie had completed and passed the GED program. On Saturday mornings she cut hair around the neighborhood. The more she cut the better her skills were. Leon convinced her to work at a barbershop in town to advertise her work and to make some money.

She had only gone into town to buy material. She made clothes for the children and sometimes made enough to sell. The one-size-fits-all house dress, kitchen aprons, and pajama sets were popular in the area.

Nina helped her cut patterns and material since she took home economics at school. She had a niche for advertising. She loved the door-to-door sells. Sometimes men bought something for their wives or convinced them to buy something because of her reputation.

Nina made miniskirts for girls at school and usually carried three or four to school for sale. Some were designed of plaid, checkered, striped, and even polyester material. The most popular miniskirt was the blue jean skirt; the tight fit was a must for house parties.

Connie was getting more attention than Melvin. Farming was no longer the conversation of the household. Connie made enough money to give the children an allowance. She finally saved enough money to pay the tuition for cosmetology classes. Two weeks later she was pregnant.

She wanted to put an end to her dreadful life. She saw people on movies using knives or guns to end their misery. That was too painful. She thought it would be awful to experience hell twice. She knew that committing suicide meant automatic hell but hoped God would have mercy. She grabbed the first bottle of pills in the medicine cabinet and took half the bottle. Then she took a hot bath and got in bed hoping to never awake.

Occasionally one of the children walked in the bedroom to check on her. They always left remembering how exhausted she was after calling her name and hearing no response. She heard their voices but couldn't seem to open her eyes or pry herself from the bed. It was midnight when she finally opened her eyes. Melvin was standing over her. She thought, *He is more evil than I could ever imagine. He should be on another level!* She remembered *Dante's Inferno,* a book Oletha read about the different levels of hell.

When she looked in the face of her youngest child, she realized she had not died. After walking to the bathroom and picking up the bottle of pills, she read the label on back of the Bayer aspirin bottle and realized no harm had been done.

The following week while driving to meet Leon, she saw Nina getting in the car with Mr. Smith, a deacon from her church. She followed them to an abandoned house and thought about her youthful life. Tears were streaming down her face as her daughter reminded her of Necie's and Oletha's behavior as teens.

Months later she had another girl! Connie busied herself reading books while recovering. She was determined that nothing would stand in her way of completing cosmetology classes.

CHAPTER TWENTY-FOUR

Ring! Ring! Daphne was calling to tell Connie that her grandmother had died. Melvin didn't allow late-night calls. After the phone stopped ringing he removed it from the base. The next day Helen called and told Connie that Leon's momma had died from cancer.

Connie didn't go to the funeral because she didn't want to hear Melvin's mouth; instead she baked a cake and left it at her mother's house for Mr. Jones. She sneaked a call to Leon and his dad to express her sorrow.

Oletha called Connie after hearing the news. She wasn't able to come for the funeral but was sending flowers with both their names. She called Mr. Jones to express her condolences. Then she listened to him talk for hours.

He started, "I knew something was wrong the day she came home from a checkup at the doctor's office. She came home in a depressed mood but never said what was bothering her. Months had passed before she told me what the doctor said. Then we agreed to tell Leon later. We tried to defeat the illness by pretending it didn't exist. Once the treatments began, her condition progressed quickly.

"All hopes of a victory were exonerated as her body grew frail. The radiation destroyed both the good and bad cells. As I sat feeding my wife a bowl of soup one evening, Leon walked in and almost went into shock after seeing his momma looking so weak. He couldn't move; he just stood there trembling. He couldn't believe this was the once jovial lady that practically grabbed him and then playfully danced around him whenever he walked into the house.

"Oletha, that boy cried like a baby. I had to get up and calm him down. It broke his momma's heart to see him break down like that. He had to get himself together for the sake of preserving her strength. He said it was hard to digest life without his momma. As the days went on he witnessed the disease destroying his momma both physically and mentally.

"Oletha, Leon's words are still playing in my mind: 'Dad, it takes a real man to take care of his wife in her darkest hour and I love you for that. If there was ever a question as to how you feel about Momma …' He grabbed me and started crying.

"He and I took turns bathing and dressing his momma. She had a thing about cleanliness. She always said, 'Cleanliness is next to godliness.' She said it was important to be presentable in the company of others.

"When people came to visit, they were always saying how good she looked for a lady in her condition. Leon happily shared the duties of taking care of his mother. Sometimes I had to remind him that he had a family, as I witnessed him and his momma spending countless hours confirming their love. She was always saying, 'Your actions are speaking louder than your words.'

"It was a Friday evening when she gained enough strength to sit up in bed and talk. During the following week I drove her to the hospital. Leon and Daphne were sleeping in his old bedroom. Around midnight her condition worsened as she moaned from pain. I tried everything; I fluffed the pillows, massaged her legs, alternated warm and cold towels, and changed her position from side to side. I had to wake Leon and Daphne to help me get her in the car. While driving to the hospital she slipped into a state of unknown as we listened to her gibberish talk.

"Once we arrived at the hospital, she was admitted and the nurse began the process of inserting a needle to release morphine. The three of us sat praying for strength to handle her fate. It was a relief to see her resting peacefully in that hospital bed. The final hour had come a few days later. Sunday evening after all the visitors had come and gone, she quietly transitioned into another life. Her fight was over and she was free from pain."

CHAPTER TWENTY-FIVE

Daphne peered out the window anxiously. No Mr. Davenport! Friday night dinners had become routine with her grandfather. After he didn't show, Daphne phoned but got no answer. As she was pulling from the drive Leon pulled in, parked his car, and then rode with her.

Mr. Davenport's red truck was parked in the drive and lights were on inside the house. They knocked but there was no answer. Leon walked around the back and peeped through the window to see him lying across the bed. After tapping on the window and calling his name, there was no response. Leon's heart was beating faster as he thought about his momma lying in the hospital bed.

He asked Daphne about a key while profusely sweating and nervously speaking. The TV was on in the bedroom and Mr. Davenport was fully clothed. Daphne called for emergency assistance.

Helen Davenport was at home sensing something terrible. Leon took the phone and told her the bad news after nothing came out clearly from listening to Daphne.

Helen remained silent while holding the receiver. Daphne collected herself and drove to pick up her momma. Reality hit after they witnessed Mr. Davenport's stiff body being removed from the room. Mrs. Davenport didn't cry; she just kept saying, "Lord have mercy!"

Two weeks later, rumors were surfacing about Mr. Davenport's death. Some were saying his wife poisoned him for treating her so badly. Others were saying another woman poisoned him. Daphne and her momma didn't respond to the rumors; they knew he died of a heart attack and they were going to miss him.

Weeks later they thought about going over to get rid of his things and tidy the house for a sale. After driving over they started removing things from his bedroom. They pulled a large black trunk from the back of his closet. Daphne got a hammer from the shed in back to knock off the padlock.

There were stacks of money and old coins. "All this money and he was riding around in that old pickup truck!"

"Daphne!"

"I can't believe it either, Momma. He always said he wanted to teach you to drive and buy you a nice car. He hated that old Ford you bought."

Helen sat there saying, "Lord have mercy!"

CHAPTER TWENTY-SIX

Connie's children were excited about her going to school. Melvin didn't say much but she didn't give him a reason to complain. She fixed him and the children a hot breakfast every morning. Once everybody left, she washed and fed the baby before putting her to bed. Then she tidied the house and washed the laundry. The remaining hours were spent reading until she fell asleep.

Meanwhile Oletha had completed her studies at the university and was working. She was sharing an apartment with a friend she met at the university. She and Steve were still in a long-distance relationship.

Her roommate was always throwing away old newspapers with red circles in the employment section. At one time Steve had considered moving there but lately he couldn't imagine living anywhere other than the South. He didn't have a problem finding work. There was always the need for a repairman to work on air conditioners and refrigerators.

One morning he went to the home of an elderly couple. As their daughter sat reading a magazine in front of the television there was a knock on the door. Steve thought he was at the wrong address after she opened the door. He remembered talking to a little ole lady a few days ago. "I'm the repairman looking for 7526 Eden Falls Road."

"This is it! The dryer is this way." Steve followed the young lady to the laundry room. *She has an ass on her!* The young lady waited while still holding the magazine to her face. Steve felt her eyes resting on him so he made sure to flex his muscles.

After finishing he needed a piece of clothing to test the heat of the dryer. *Look at the tits on this chic! She is bold as hell!* He hadn't met anyone this bold since Oletha. He stood in shock with his mouth hanging open after she pulled off her shirt and tossed it inside the dryer.

After she instructed him to reach and get what he wanted, he smeared her tits over his face and then wet them with warm moisture. The young lady unzipped his trousers to discover something nice inside. Eventually there was an exact fit as he moved in a way to make her moan and groan. After showering and getting dressed, she told Steve her name and apologized for coming on so aggressively. He said it was no problem because he enjoyed every minute of it.

She unzipped his trousers again and wet his dick in a way he had only experienced with Oletha. "Damn, girl, you're the shit!" Then he played with the opening of her tunnel, which obviously a good spot, as she moved rather strangely.

After she walked Steve to his truck, she touched the area of joy. "I was wondering if and when I'll see you again."

"Now you're talking my language!" She hopped in his lap and began squirming. Steve joined in and used his muscular arms to lift her up and down.

"I'll be home around five after I pick up my son."

"Son?"

"Yeah, he's three years old."

Damn, I didn't know she had a son! Shoot, with pussy this good I don't care if she has three sons. This freak is the shit! Steve pulled off singing, while replacing the lyrics with his own words. He had not been this happy since Oletha was home a few months ago.

Steve had always acted like a savage beast whenever Oletha came home but lately he was acting like a docile dog. She asked, "Steve, who's the lucky bitch?"

"What?"

"Who is she?"

After making up several excuses, he confessed there was someone new in his life. Then he tried to accuse her of having someone up North. Oletha didn't fall for that reversed psychology shit. "So how did you meet her, Steve?"

"Why, Oletha? Does it matter?"

"So how is she in bed?"

"Ah, she's all right!" *Hell, that freak is off the chain. I get a hard-on just thinking about that piece of ass and the way she sucks my dick!*

She reminded Steve that she knew the signs too well. Then she told him about the time her roommate's fiancé was cheating. "I was at a house party with people busily chatting, playing cards, watching movies, and mixing drinks when I started gyrating to the beat. In walked my roommate's fiancé while I was demonstrating a popular dance from the South.

"My colleague walked him around to meet everybody. I spoke and kept dancing. It didn't bother me that he was cheating but it bothered him. He couldn't enjoy the party after seeing me.

"A few weeks later, I walked in to find my roommate crying. She said her fiancé was cheating. I couldn't believe he had gone that long without being caught. Then I tried to convince her it was probably his first time. She said that's exactly what he said."

"Huh?"

"Yeah, he said it was his first time and she didn't mean anything to him." *This fool ain't too bad! They all use that same weak-ass excuse? She must marry him! I mean he's a nervous wreck when he screws up, so that means he does have a conscience! Most guys screw up and don't give a damn.*

"Maybe he's telling the truth."

"What? I can't believe you're siding with him."

"I'm just saying sometimes guys do tell the truth. We just don't know when they're telling the truth. I don't think they know when they're telling the truth. So maybe you should give him another chance."

CHAPTER TWENTY-SEVEN

Daphne was in twelfth grade and interested in a guy from school. Jamie played on the school's baseball team. He was nervous about inviting her to a baseball game. "We have a game Thursday and I was wondering if you could stay."

"I might be able to do that! Will you be playing or riding the pine?"

Jamie smiled and said, "I hope the coach lets me play."

Later that day Jamie was walking with another player on his team. "I saw that."

"What?"

"Daphne! I saw you giving her the eye!"

"She's hot!"

"Yeah, but I don't think she's into the sex thing. Rumor has it, she's still a virgin."

"Well, maybe I'll be the chosen one."

"I wouldn't count on it if I were you. This dude on the football team said she's a tease. He said they were in the back of his parents' van kissing when she let him suck her tits and finger her pussy. She got him all worked up and then decided she wasn't ready."

"I invited her to our game Thursday."

"I knew it, man! I knew you were giving her the eye! What did she say?"

"She said she'll think about it. Why don't you help me and give her a ride home!"

"What about my girl?"

"I'm sure she'll understand."

"I don't know, man. It's not that easy to convince a black girl that nothing's going on with you and another girl riding in your car. Is your girl staying for the game?"

"Probably. Well she'll see that it's me Daphne's interested in and not you."

Daphne and a friend stayed after school to watch the baseball game as she searched frantically for Jamie on the field. She didn't see him anywhere. Her friend finally spotted him and then pointed him out; he was on the pitcher's mound.

After the game he and a teammate walked over to where they were standing. Daphne congratulated him on a great performance and then teased him about his modest attitude toward the game. Jamie and Daphne exchanged numbers and later talked for hours before going to bed.

Daphne wanted advice about how far to go with Jamie. *If I had a relationship with Connie I'm sure she would be more understanding than Momma, who is set in her ole southern ways. I'll get some advice from Aunt Necie.*

After church and Sunday dinner, I began mentioning boys to Aunt Necie. "Okay, is this something serious?"

"No, not really, I just want some advice."

"Are you sure it's your Aunt Necie's advice you want?" said Jeff's wife.

"And what are you trying to say, Tracey?"

"I don't know if baby girl can handle your advice. She might need something a little mild."

"Well, thanks for the compliment and thanks for recognizing my talent."

"Since both of you have experience, I can use some advice from both of my aunts. Jamie plays on the school's baseball team."

"Wait a minute! Did you say baseball team? Baseball is a white boy sport."

"Does it matter that he's white Aunt Tracey? He likes me and we've been talking on the phone."

"Well, I'm going to let you handle this Necie. I think I'll take a seat next to my little niece and get some advice myself because this one is out of my league and out of my race."

"Okay, Daphne! Do his parents know about you?"

"Sort of."

"Huh?"

"What I mean is they know he talks to a Daphne but they don't know Daphne's black. Momma knows that I talk to a Jamie but has never asked what color he is. So what should I do?"

"I think you should talk to him because you guys are not serious enough to get married or anything. You haven't slept with him, have you?"

"No, ma'am. I'm still a virgin!"

"Will somebody please slap me?" said Tracey. "Pour me a glass of that cold tea! It is hot in here!"

"Come here. I'm so proud of you!"

"That's double for me! I know who ain't a virgin!"

"Who?"

"Your sister Nina. She ain't been a virgin since she was twelve."

"Ooooo, you should be ashamed of yourself Tracey."

"No, Necie, she should be ashamed of herself. You know I'm telling the truth and so does Daphne. Am I right?"

"Well, she's not a virgin but I don't know how old she was when she stopped being a virgin."

"I love my niece. But that girl is so hot that she probably carries a dick around in her purse in case she feels the urge to 'get down on it!'"

Helen Davenport walked in and asked what all the commotion was about and then looked to see her daughter-in-law, Tracey acting a fool. "Oh, I see somebody is entertaining ya'll in here!" Then she grabbed something and went back outside.

Two weeks later there was another baseball game. Daphne and Jamie were alone in the school's parking lot following the Friday night baseball game. They were talking on the back of his truck. He began kissing Daphne all over. Within minutes she was moaning. She didn't expect Jamie to make her body shiver. She hadn't experienced that since she hung out with Nina and the preacher.

When Jamie asked her to please him, Daphne refused. Then she heard Aunt Necie's voice: *If you're hesitant about carrying out a request, don't, because you'll regret it later.* Jamie got upset and accused Daphne of being a "dick teaser." This pissed her off and she jumped in her car and left.

CHAPTER TWENTY-EIGHT

Connie had finished her cosmetology classes and was cutting hair at a barbershop in town. She enjoyed being away from home and making her own money. She also enjoyed the freedom to make decisions without Melvin's input.

Daphne had heard that Connie worked at the shop from students at school. She wanted her hair fixed but was nervous about going, so she asked Nina to go with her. Daphne and Nina were surprised at Connie's request for payment. *How could she?* It was a quiet ride home, as they were both in disbelief about Connie's behavior.

Meanwhile, Helen Davenport was phoning a neighbor for a lift to the doctor. She was experiencing a shortness of breath and a tingling in her left arm. Daphne walked in fussing about Connie. She kept asking her mother what she had done to make Connie treat her so badly. She couldn't figure out why Connie was so coldhearted toward her. Helen and Daphne were shouting when Helen grabbed her chest.

Daphne called for emergency assistance after her mother collapsed.

Daphne called her dad while sitting in the waiting room of the hospital. On their way home she told him what led to her mother collapsing. Then she asked how he could have ever loved a hateful person like Connie. Leon explained that Connie was nothing like she is now.

He said sometimes the company you keep will turn you bitter inside. In Connie's case it was marrying someone who already had a tainted heart. Leon apologized to Daphne for feeling so empty inside.

After phoning Necie about her mother in the hospital, Charla, Jeff, and Sammy came to check on her as well. Daphne stayed out of sight when she found out that Connie was coming to the hospital. After days of attempting to stabilize a fluctuating blood pressure Helen Davenport was released from the hospital.

Months later Daphne was graduating from high school. Leon and his wife took the Davenports to dinner. It was Saturday night, Helen apologized to Leon for the first time in the midst of his wife, his daddy, Necie, Nina, Daphne, Sammy, Charla, and Jeff.

"I'm sorry for everything. Will you please forgive me?"

Nina and Daphne were sitting in service Sunday morning after hanging out late last night. They were looking a bit confused after fighting the battle of sleep. Ms. Davenport's rule was that you had to attend church no matter how late you were out the night before. Sleep was no longer the enemy after Nina spotted something interesting.

"I like that!" Nina said, "Your preacher has it going on!" Nina followed members to greet Reverend Pete after service. She introduced herself as Daphne's sister and

Helen's granddaughter. Reverend Pete couldn't resist looking at her smooth brown legs coming from under the plaid minidress.

After dinner and a nap following service, Nina asked Daphne to give her a ride to Reverend Pete's house. "Are you serious?"

"Do I look like I'm playing?"

"No, but I hope you are! And where will the Reverend's wife be when I'm dropping you off at his house?"

"He said the choir won't be returning until tomorrow night."

"Where did you get so much information?"

"On the way from the bathroom I stopped at the door with 'Pastor's Study' written on it."

"You didn't!"

"I knocked, he said come in, and I told him how I enjoyed the service. Then I told him about my troubles. That's when he invited me over for counseling tonight."

CHAPTER TWENTY-NINE

Helen Davenport retired from work after Daphne convinced her to live off the money her grandfather had left. She bought a new car and then split the money with her children. Jeff started teaching his momma how to drive. His wife laughed after he came home, sighing from her progress.

"That's what you should have been doing all summer instead of hanging out in the streets." It was the end of summer before his momma was ready to get her driving license.

Daphne was interested in becoming a nurse after watching the nurses in the hospital. She volunteered at the hospital while working a part-time job at a neighborhood grocery store. The manager asked her to stay on once school began if it didn't conflict with her classes.

"Momma, Nina and I are leaving to hang out with some friends."

"Did you tell Nina about your friend from work?"

"No, Momma!" Momma thought Matthew was nice

because he let me have my way at work. He was the manager at the store.

"Nina, most managers are white!"

"Daphne, you're dating a white guy!"

"When will I get to meet him?"

"You will."

"How about tonight?"

"Maybe."

"We can go over there first."

"See what you started, Momma."

"I thought you wanted your sister to meet your boyfriend."

"Momma, he's not my boyfriend. He's just a friend."

"Anybody who stays on the phone as much as you two has to be more than friends!"

Nina admired how her sister talked to guys on the phone. Nina said, "Excuse me, sis. I didn't hear anything about sex."

"We haven't known each other that long. It's only been three or four months."

"Three or four months! Are you kidding? I've never talked to a guy that long without giving him something sweet. Why are you always in a hurry to give up the goods, Nina?"

"Daphne, I discovered a long time ago that sex is the only reason guys like girls."

"But what if you don't really like him?"

"I'm too young to get married so why should I be concerned about whether or not a guy likes me?" *Maybe I'm better off without Connie because my sister's thoughts are scary. Poor thing, with a momma and a daddy at home!*

Daphne and Nina drove to find Reverend Pete's house before driving to meet her friend. "Hi, Matthew!"

"Hi, Daph!" *Daph, what the hell? She didn't tell me he was a fine white boy! I know his ass is freaky as hell!* "This is my sister Nina."

"Hi, Nina, I've heard a lot about you."

"Oh, really? Well, I haven't heard anything about you. Is this your place?"

"Yeah."

"This is tight!"

"Glad you like it."

"Let me get you ladies something cold to drink."

"I'll take a coke on the rocks, if you don't mind."

"Daphne, what would you like?" "I'll take the same."

"So Daphne how did you two hook up?"

"After giving me a ride home one night from work we started talking. "

"To be a white boy he's kind of cute."

"You think so?"

"Yeah and I bet he can eat some pussy! "

"I wouldn't know about that Nina."

"Well you need to find out if the saying is true. I heard that white boys started the oral thang! You know the brothas didn't think that shit was cool until later."

Daphne and Nina sat chatting with Matthew after he returned from the kitchen with their sodas. When it was time for Nina's date, Matthew suggested Daphne drop her sister off and come back to wait at his place. "Are you sure I won't be interrupting your evening?"

"I'll see you in a few minutes Daph."

"So what do you think Sis?"

"I think you need to find out what's going on in the bedroom before you invest too much time."

"I should have known you were thinking something like that."

Daphne and Nina arrived at Reverend Pete's house. *Ding! Dong! Ding!* After the door opened, Nina waved at her sister to leave.

"Hello, miss."

"Hi, Reverend Pete. It's dark in here! Did somebody forget to pay the light bill? But if you're okay sitting in the dark I can adjust."

"I was in my office reading over some papers."

"That cologne sure smells good!" Nina followed him through the house and pinched his bum. Then he took a detour to his bedroom.

"Excuse me, this don't look like an office!"

"Well, with the friendly gesture you made, I thought we should skip the office tour and get to something more interesting."

"That sounds nice." Nina helped the reverend take off his shirt. Reverend Pete's hands moved slowly up Nina's legs, caressing the muscular tone of her calf and then her thighs. "Oops! I forgot to put on panties."

Reverend Pete's heart was pounding as he maneuvered the short khaki skirt down those young firm legs; he had never witnessed such perfection. Her bum reminded him of tires with too much air. He lifted the bum to watch it jerk as it fell in place.

Nina had the pleasure of making her bum vibrate. "Lord have mercy! Miss, you're gonna make my blood pressure shoot up!" Reverend Pete had never been with someone

Nina's age but he had no regrets as he devoured her warm body.

What he didn't know was that he was stirring in a hornet's nest. Nina reached to feel the size of his dick and then assisted him with the right slot. "Reverend, will you make me shout? Or make me speak in tongues?" After an ongoing clashing battle, he and Nina found satisfaction.

"Break over. It's time to get back to work!" Nina and the reverend sat in the middle of his leather sofa. She moved in a rhythmic pattern as if stirring in a bowl. Nina took her time torturing Reverend Pete.

Daphne drove back to Matthew's house while thinking about her sister's life. She realized Connie was nothing more than her sister's parent. She was not involved in Nina's life either. Matthew was glad she hadn't changed her mind about returning to his place. The room where they sat watching a movie was only lit from the light of the television. After watching a heated love scene, Matthew and Daphne started kissing, and out of nowhere came the arms of an octopus. He quickly engulfed her body as she effortlessly surrendered.

He picked up the glass of red wine and began pouring it onto her navel. Matthew caught the wine before it reached the most delicate area of her body. Daphne couldn't explain what she was experiencing. Matthew worked vigorously to insert the throbbing object inside the tunnel. She was glad he erupted. She didn't know how much longer she could stand him biting on her breasts.

Matthew carefully rubbed soap in the most profound area while on his knees as warm water ran over his face. Daphne faced the shower walls as Matthew indulged in forceful strokes. After returning to watch the movie, he fell asleep in her lap.

Daphne was supposed to collect Nina from Reverend Pete's house at a certain time but decided to give her sister more time. That's just what Nina and Reverend Pete were doing—they were working overtime! Nina had tied him to the bed and even blindfolded him while pretending he was a human piñata.

Reverend Pete was exhausted, but Nina refused to let him stop until he freed all her demons. He was finally gasping for air! "Are those demons gone yet, miss?"

"Yes, Reverend!"

"It's about time because I have run out of ammunition!"

"You were great, Reverend!"

"I'm just glad I freed all those demons."

Reverend Pete smiled as Nina stroked his ego. "The first lady better recognize what she has here."

"Okay, miss, let's get dressed so we won't surprise anybody."

"Shall we shower first?"

"Sounds like you're up to some trickery."

CHAPTER THIRTY

Mr. Jones had grown weary. He tried to keep busy with an overflow of automobiles to repair. He rarely ate a hot meal. Death was weighing heavily on his mind whenever he thought about his late wife.

Leon often stopped to lend a hand. After watching his dad sit alone in front of the television eating a sandwich and then chasing it with a glass of iced tea, he suggested to his dad that he should find a female friend. Mr. Jones didn't respond. Leon repeated, "Dad, you need a companion to remind you that life is worth living!"

"Son, I must look pretty pitiful."

"This house could use a woman's touch. I know you loved Momma and miss her but we have to keep living. That's what living life to the fullest is all about. I'm man enough to want to see you happy again."

Weeks later Leon drove over and unexpectedly found his dad in bed. "It's noon. Why are you still in bed?"

"Son, I decided to rest and take it easy today."

"Have you been up at all?"

"I got up to take care of my hygiene and then got back in bed after I felt sort of dizzy."

"Why didn't you call me or something?"

"Son, I'm all right!"

"You don't look all right, and why are you sweating? Come on, Dad, and get dressed. I'm taking you to the doctor."

Mr. Jones was checked ahead of others who were waiting due to his temperature and age. He had pneumonia and neglected medical attention at its onset. He was admitted to the hospital. Leon had always kept in contact with Oletha and decided to give her a call. He remembered how she was always fond of his dad's company, and he seemed to have enjoyed her as well.

Oletha made it down South just as Mr. Jones was being released from the hospital. She refused to take Leon's money; she said there was never a price for helping a friend. Mr. Jones was happy to have Oletha there. *It's a shame for an older man to look so damn handsome when he's sick.* Oletha had planned to spend three weeks between her mother's house and Mr. Jones's house.

Her nosy Aunt Linda couldn't rest after hearing Oletha was in town staying with Mr. Jones. She remembered the time she went over to dry her clothes and saw Mr. Jones leaving her sister's house. *So it was Bessie's daughter he was checking on and all this time I thought it was Bessie. He had a lot of nerve visiting her in broad daylight while his wife was away taking care of her sickly mother! I wonder if Bessie knew about them. I should have known something was going on. Every time I saw Helen's daughter with that Jones boy, Oletha was always hanging around!* Aunt Linda picked up the phone with a new topic for today's gossiping session.

Oletha fixed Mr. Jones soup and administered his medicines. She slept in an oversized chair near his bed. During the night he looked to see her resting and felt lucky to have her there. Before dozing off he always thanked God for sending him an angel.

Bam! Bam! Bam! Oletha walked to greet a guest of Mr. Jones. She opened the door to find Aunt Linda standing with a large pot in her hands. Oletha had a toothbrush and face towel in hand. "Hello, Aunt Linda!"

"How is Mr. Jones?"

"He's doing better and I'm expecting him to return to his old self any day!"

I just bet you are!

"What's in the pot?"

"Some homemade soup for Mr. Jones. Is he up?"

"Yes, ma'am. Mr. Jones, are you decent? Somebody is here to see you."

Oletha's aunt was pointed to the bedroom, and she went to shower and get dressed. Mr. Jones was sitting in the oversized chair where she slept sipping on a cup of warm tea. Aunt Linda started chatting while her reckless eyes roamed the room for evidence. When she didn't see anything, she asked to use the restroom. She was unlucky to find nothing there. She was desperate to see something, anything that said Oletha and Mr. Jones had something going on. She noticed a blanket across the back of the chair and asked Mr. Jones if he was still shivering at night. He said the blanket was for Oletha when she sat in his room until he fell asleep at night.

After Aunt Linda didn't find what she was hoping to see, she bid Mr. Jones farewell. She got lost on her way out of the three-bedroom house. She saw Oletha's bags in a room where the bed was slightly unmade. She opened the door to the third bedroom to see a room too neat for anybody to have slept in last night.

Oletha opened the bathroom door to startle her aunt. She asked if she had found Mr. Jones doing well and everything in order. "Oh, yes, I was trying to find my way out. Mr. Jones is a fine-looking man even when he's sick."

"You think so?"

"Don't you?"

"I haven't paid any attention since he's old enough to be my daddy." *I bet your nosy ass was trying to see if there were signs of me sleeping with Mr. Jones. If you want to see something, you should ride over to Ms. Lena Jackson's house or Ms. Loretta Stamps's house; I bet you'll find something interesting.*

"Most young folks don't have time to take care of their elders, and you came all the way down to take care of a man who isn't your father."

"Anything for a friend!"

"A friend?"

"Leon asked me to help him take care of his father and offered to pay." *I know you will have to pay your children to come and check on your ole nosy ass and I'm not so sure they'll come then.*

"See you later, Oletha!"

"Bye, Aunt Linda! Tell my uncle hello!" Oletha finished dressing and fixed Mr. Jones a bowl of her aunt's delicious soup. Then they sat eating soup and watching television while chatting about each other's lives.

Oletha stopped at the local store before driving to her mother's house. While preparing dinner she phoned to check on Mr. Jones. He assured her that he was feeling stronger and to take her time. Leon walked in and was happy to see his father sitting up watching television. He grabbed the phone to tell Oletha that whatever she was doing is working.

Ms. Bessie arrived home wondering what the nice aroma was. Oletha greeted her with a man-gripping hug and kiss. "Mom, I've missed being here with you! I fixed you one of my mouthwatering dishes my roommate cooks sometimes."

"It sure smells delicious!"

"Wait until you taste it!"

"What is it?"

"It's curry chicken, steamed broccoli with a sprinkle of cheese, naan bread, and a glass of rose wine."

"Wine!"

"It's red so it's good for you."

"Well, haven't we learned good housekeeping skills!"

"Oletha, you must be entertaining some lucky man."

"I have some friends but nobody special like Steve, if that's what you mean. I haven't met Mr. Right."

"I'm sure when you find him he won't be leaving with these skills."

"I hope you're right, Mom."

"What about you? How is your love life?"

"Oh, it's the same. I'm still dating the guy who drives the white pickup truck."

"I thought you two would have gotten married by now."

"Oh did you? Don't think he hasn't asked. I'm just a bit skeptical after I remember how your dad up and left. I'm not sure I'll have the strength to go through that again."

"How is Mr. Jones?"

"He's better. You know, for an older man he sure is handsome."

"I'm surprised you were able to get inside that house with so many women trying to get in."

"Oh really!"

"Yeah, women have been after that man since his wife died. I guess that son keeps them away! I guess he trusts you being there with his father unless he's keeping you in sight for himself."

"No, Momma, I had a thing for Leon a long time ago. We're strictly friends!"

"I think it's great how you and Leon remained friends after Connie left ya'll. Oletha, have you seen her since you've been here?"

"No, Momma, not yet."

"I sure hate that she made a mess of things with that Melvin."

"Momma, it was her choice so she'll have to live with her decision."

"I worry about Daphne, the daughter she refuses to acknowledge."

Oletha tidied the kitchen and spent a few hours chatting with her momma until she got into bed. Then she drove back to Mr. Jones's house. After opening the door there were faint sounds coming from the back room. Hesitantly, she announced that she was walking back. Mr. Jones was falling asleep in bed with the television on.

"So how is Ms. Bessie?"

"She's doing fine and she asked about you too. I think I had one too many glasses of wine."

"Wine!"

"Yeah, I shared a glass of my favorite wine with my favorite lady."

Oletha went missing for about an hour, soaking in

some nice lavender bath petals from a porcelain vase. Mr. Jones welcomed the soft smell of her body as she returned to nestle in the oversized chair. After getting permission to snuggle under the covers, Oletha felt something familiar as his hands roamed freely. She was a bit excited from the wine. They remembered what it was like to hold each other. Oletha and Mr. Jones entertained each other all night. They got up around noon.

After the sun came up, she fixed lunch and tidied his room. He was no longer the sickly man she was caring for earlier. While taking clothes from the dryer, Mr. Jones stopped to help. Moments later her dress was up around her waist while he was excitedly breathing behind her.

Mr. Jones perspired so much Oletha began to worry. He assured her he was fine and she was doing a good job of forcing the impurities from his body. She fixed him a warm bath and sat next to the basin. Then he thanked her for bringing romance back into his bedroom years ago when he thought his wife was no longer interested.

Oletha's hand sank into the bath and grabbed the magic between his legs that always brought her joy. Mr. Jones's hands were lost in her shirt. He found the valuable jewels and took his time going from left to right moistening both. Oletha stood and dropped her skirt. *Damn! Bring those T-backs here!*

"Dad! Dad!"

"Oh, shit, it's Leon!" Oletha grabbed her skirt and pulled it up while running into the bedroom closet. There she sat pretending to organize Mr. Jones's shoes among other things when Leon walked in.

"Where's Dad?"

"Oh, he's in the bath getting rid of more impurities."

"You're cleaning his closet too? I'll have to pay you big-time for all of this."

"No bother, just make sure your wife releases you if I ever get sick."

"No problem. She's glad you were able to oblige our request since she had used all her vacation time. Hi, Dad!"

"Hi, son!"

"How are you feeling today?"

"Just fine!"

"I just stopped to see if you needed anything."

"I think we're okay. You can check with Oletha to see if she needs anything."

"You sure are doing a lot of sweating! I guess that's what Oletha meant by getting rid of the impurities! You almost sound like yourself again."

"What do you mean?"

"Your voice sounds stronger, and your skin looks younger. Oletha, thank you! Well, Dad, since you're doing fine and Oletha is busy doing her thing, I'm on my way to work. Oletha, I'm leaving money on the kitchen counter."

"If you insist, Leon."

Oletha and Mr. Jones waited until they heard Leon slam his car door and pull away before they continued with their activity. She locked the bedroom door and the bathroom door. The curtains were pulled to make the room darker.

Oletha pulled off everything except her red lace thong that Mr. Jones instructed her to leave on and stepped into the bath. He positioned his body to allow her to sit on his thighs. Then she massaged his dick while he sucked her breasts. There was too much excitement as he lifted her from his thighs and turned her in the opposite direction.

As her hands and knees rested on the floor of the basin,

he enjoyed playing with the string of the T-back. He pulled over the lace and allowed his tongue to search the treasure chest for the most precious jewel.

CHAPTER THIRTY-ONE

Daphne and Matthew were making wedding plans. They were also exploring the idea of moving up North. Daphne was ready to start a new life with the man second to her dad. She couldn't wait to leave a place of so many bad memories.

Oletha was eager to assist them with a smooth transition to a place she now considered home. She found a piece of inexpensive property primed for development by the newly elected mayor. After describing the property to Matthew, he was interested in having a look.

Meanwhile, Nina was in her senior year of high school entertaining a football player. Her reputation was as popular with the youth as with some adults throughout the community. It was no bother to her; the more the merrier. The football player had a girlfriend, but if Nina showed up he was all hers; he didn't want to risk the chance of missing out on something exciting.

Nina was enjoying her senior year. She had never been as popular as she was this year. She was in great demand.

After worship service on Sundays, Deacon Smith worked at befriending Melvin and Connie. While other members paid to gather goods from his garden, Melvin could gather without paying.

When the deacon's wife questioned his generosity toward Melvin and Connie, he quoted the scripture about giving freely. He convinced her they should uphold the biblical teachings of giving until it hurts.

Their daughter gives until it hurts me to perform in bed with you. That girl's cunt grabs my dick like it's the last one around. I get chills just thinking about her. Sometime I want to pass her my dues instead of putting them on the offering table.

Melvin and Connie were excited about Nina's graduation. She earned their trust after making the honor roll occasionally and working a part-time job. Their little girl had grown up. They were just clueless about her grown-up activities.

Daphne and Matthew realized Nina had the behavior of a sex addict. She couldn't get rid of sexual urges without partners. She had even expressed to Daphne how she sometimes had relations three times a day and not always with the same partner. Daphne asked people in the medical field if there was a diagnosis for people who had an overactive sex drive. "Is it possible for someone to be a sex addict?"

Her teacher was planning to present her with the biology award during graduation. He worked with Nina twice a week after school. When other teachers witnessed them working so hard, they supported his decision.

The classroom closet became a lover's den. Nina was so demanding that she sometimes took a break before starting their session. She couldn't calm the beast inside. She took advantage of the empty closet that housed antiquated choir robes. When and if she was satisfied, they returned to the assignment.

Nina was eager to join her sister at the university. They were both excited about becoming registered nurses. People were often mimicking how nice it was for two sisters to have a common interest. Melvin didn't like Nina being identified as following the footsteps of Daphne. Nina resented his comments but didn't bother disputing because he would never change his evil ways toward a sister she admired.

Nina never wasted her time on nonproductive situations; she always busied herself with something fun and exciting. One night after leaving a high school football game with a co-worker she decided to spend the night. After being introduced to her co-worker's brother he became too excited.

"This has to be the same Nina."

"Guys from school are always talking about some girl named Nina. And this Nina is fine as hell!" After he kept starring, Nina knew he was interested and snuck into his bedroom during the night. She didn't waste any time getting acquainted with his manly skills.

"It's true! That's one bad ass girl!" He finally got a chance to experience the girl his sister often talked about from work which turned out to be the same girl the guys often bragged about at school.

Nina said this year was her year. She said it was a pleasure to graduate from high school without any screwups. Out of her many sexual encounters, she had never faced a conflict with either a spouse or a girlfriend of any lover. She was as smooth as Mother Nature transitioning through the seasons of spring, summer, winter, and fall.

CHAPTER THIRTY-TWO

Three months later Nina graduated from high school. Daphne didn't attend the graduation. She had finally removed all thoughts of attempting a relationship with Connie and Melvin. She and Nina were celebrating later. Nina got a lot of gifts from people at school as well as church and a few anonymous acquaintances. After spending time with her siblings and parents, she met Daphne and Matthew.

They had planned a gathering for Nina and invited Necie, Jeff and Tracey, Charla and Rufus, friends from school, her daddy, and of course her momma, Helen. After Jeff left to carry his momma home, the younger ladies were alone and crying from laughter after Nina shared moments of entertaining lovers. Tracey laughed until she was crying. Then she asked Necie how she trained her niece so well. Necie responded, "It's in the bloodline."

Nina spent the night with Daphne. She received several phone calls throughout the day but her sister demanded she disregard them all because today was their day. Nina shared a bottle of champagne with her sister as they sat and talked until their eyes were too heavy to keep open.

Daphne ran a hot bath, and then she and Nina sat in the water sharing laughter at happy moments and tears during the sad moments. Matthew went to bed; he knew they needed time to vent their frustrations from many years of pain.

After drying their bodies and dressing for bed, Daphne applied lotion to her sister's back as she shared her most intimate feelings about their mother. They were up for hours crying over years of pain. They both discovered that the other was experiencing the same amount of pain, but dealing with it in a different manner. After Daphne walked into her bedroom and saw that Matthew had fallen asleep, she returned to the guest room with Nina. They resumed their chatter until quiet yawns demanded their attention.

Eventually they fell asleep. For the first time in years they slept like babies. Daphne held Nina as if she were the comforter, and Nina's body illustrated surrender. Nina had never talked about her frustrations; she had always sought comfort in a lover.

The following day, the two sisters awoke to find a note that was left on the kitchen table saying to call. She smiled and picked up the phone to call. Matthew instructed her and Nina to meet him for lunch. They rushed to dress while engaging in small talk. Daphne happily drove her sister to meet her soon-to-be husband at their favorite breakfast place.

Matthew teased them about sleeping arm in arm like babies. They smiled and said he was welcome to join them. He reminded Nina that he did consider but decided against the idea when he thought about her mistaking him for one of her lovers.

CHAPTER THIRTY-THREE

"I'm glad you're here. Remove everything and lie down. Lift your arms while I check carefully in both areas. No lumps or humps. They're so fucking beautiful. I miss these tits and my favorite little perky friends."

"Did you want to be a doctor before taking a job at the university?"

"I thought about becoming a specialist in this area. Tell the doctor again where it hurts. My patient feels so soft and tastes so sweet."

"How about the more potent stuff, Doc?"

"Again? Give me a minute to catch my breath! I can't let campus security find a motionless corpse belonging to the university's biology professor."

The alarm clock is sounding as Nina awakes with a smile about a night with her professor. A few months at the university was long enough to replace old lovers. There was always something exciting going on in the biology department.

There was a pause in the semester when a demon

escaped with free rein to torment! Without warning Nina experienced something other than the usual throbbing dick. The room was smoldering hot and spun out of control as she tried to get dressed for class. She was forced back in bed after salty saliva filled her mouth. Soon she was heaving and luckily made it to the toilet.

Meanwhile, Daphne was concerned about her sister's absence because she never missed a meal. After leaving the café where she ate lunch, she phoned Nina. It was scary walking into the dorm room and finding her sister in bed. Nina had no history of sleeping in, especially alone. Then she gave her sister details of an earlier scene. They agreed the food from last night's buffet didn't agree with them.

"When was your last menstrual cycle?" They shared the same thought as their eyes met. "I don't want a baby! I finished high school without any screwups! Hell, I'm not in love! What will guys think of me? I can't walk around campus looking like a blimp!"

"Calm down, it's not the end of the world."

"That's easy for you to say."

"Who's the father?"

"'Who's the father?' What kind of question is that?"

Nina was hysterical!